18/30

KT-910-522

£2
90

The aims of
education
restated

By the same author:

Towards a Compulsory Curriculum
Philosophers as Educational Reformers (with P. Gordon)

The aims of education restated

John White

ROUTLEDGE & KEGAN PAUL
London, Boston and Henley

First published in 1982
by Routledge & Kegan Paul Ltd
39 Store Street, London WC1E 7DD,
9 Park Street, Boston, Mass. 02108, USA and
Broadway House, Newtown Road,
Henley-on-Thames, Oxon RG9 1EN

Set in Times by Computacomp (UK) Ltd
Fort William, Scotland
and printed in Great Britain by Redwood Burn Ltd
Trowbridge, Wiltshire

© John White 1982
No part of this book may be reproduced in
any form without permission from the
publisher, except for the quotation of brief
passages in criticism

Library of Congress Cataloging in Publication Data

White, John Ponsford.
  The aims of education restated.
  Bibliography: p.
  Includes index.
  1. Education – Aims and objectives. I. Title.
LB41.W58   370'.11   81–14385
ISBN 0-7100-0941-0   AACR2
ISBN 0-7100-0998-4 (pbk.)

Contents

Acknowledgments vii
Preface ix
1 **Introduction** 1
  A revised concept of education
  Are aims necessary?
2 **Intrinsic aims** 9
  Types of justification
  Excellence and selection
  Conclusion
3 **The good of the pupil** 23
  Introduction
  Basic goods
  Intrinsic goods
  Pupil-centred education: the two-fold tasks
4 **The good of society (1): economic, moral and pupil-centred aims** 61
  Economic aims and pupil-centred aims
  Moral aims and pupil-centred aims
5 **The good of society (2): moral aims in their economic and political aspects** 104
  Moral aims and economic aims
  Citizenship as an aim
6 **The educated man** 121
  A sketch of his achievements
  Problems of objectivity and indoctrination
  Childhood education and lifelong education
  Different aims for different pupils?
7 **The realisation of aims** 140
  Socio-economic conditions

Educational means
(1) The ethos of the community
(2) Schools
(3) Other educational institutions
A utopian theory?
Notes 170
Bibliography 173
Index 175

Acknowledgments

I would like to thank those of my MA students at the London Institute of Education who heard or read earlier drafts of this book and under pressure of whose criticisms I reconstructed my main argument, sometimes in a radical way. I am grateful, too, for comments on chapter 3, both from members of the Philosophy of Education Society, to whom I read papers in Reading, Exeter, Birmingham and London, and from members of the Policies Research Group in Philosophy of Education at the London Institute.

The comments both of Professor Richard Peters and of Routledge's anonymous reader proved very helpful in the final stages of writing and I would like to thank them warmly for the care they took and the judiciousness of their comments.

My colleague Graham Haydon kindly read and commented on one of the early drafts. To my wife and colleague, Pat White, I owe an inexpressible debt. This partly concerns the content of the book, since the basic conception of educating pupils for membership of a participatory democracy has been heavily influenced by her thought. To her critical acumen and constant encouragement through all the writings and rewritings, I owe almost everything. I would like to say a word of thanks and apology, too, to our daughter, Louise, who has had to put up with a lot of talk within the family over the last few years about the aims of education, despite the fact that the three things she dislikes most are philosophy, education and politics!

My final thanks are to Mrs E. M. Simpson and Bernadette Cifuentes for their help in preparing the typescript.

Preface

This is not by any means a long book, but it is the longest piece of work on what the aims of education should be that has been published, to my knowledge, since ... shall we say since Whitehead's *Aims of Education* of 1929? Not really. Whitehead's book is a collection of essays on various subjects, only one of which is on the topic in the title. It may sound odd, in view of the importance of the issue, but, unless I am mistaken, there just has not been as yet any book-length investigation of priorities among educational aims.

This causes me some last minute nervousness as I write this preface. Perhaps there are only too telling reasons why no one has attempted this. Is the topic too impossibly vast, too densely interconnected with fundamental and ramifying questions about ultimate values, the good of society, mankind's place in the cosmos, to be tractable in less than thirty-two closely printed volumes? Or is it, on the contrary, that there is *nothing* whatsoever to say: that there's no point in discussing what the aims of education should be, either because there aren't any, or because all any such discussion could amount to would be purely subjective lucubrations?

I would prefer to think that there are other explanations. For the past twenty years at least, the keyword in writings about the content of education has been 'curriculum', not 'aims'. Under the *aegis* of the Schools Council and other bodies there has been a constant flow of projects, working papers, books and articles on all aspects of school curricula. Only gradually, it seems to me, has it become apparent that, excellent as much of this work has been in detail, it cannot stand alone without some overall picture of how the various bits and pieces should fit together, of what they are all *for*. One could, I suppose, spend a long time fashioning separate stones, which will some day be put together to make a house, without having any overall architectural conception of how the house should look. It would seem more sensible in both cases to begin from general aims and work down into particularities from there. But when it comes to social planning, of which educational planning is one example, this seems to go against the grain of the British temperament, at least in its late twentieth-century form. 'Piecemeal social engineering', to use Karl Popper's well-known phrase, is more congenial to us than working from first principles. 'Going back to square one' is not exactly seen as a recipe for social progress.

One might have thought that of all the educational disciplines, philosophy of education would have kept its head so high in the air, that general discussions of educational aims would be just what it would engage in. But until very recently it has been much more analytically orientated. It has been interested in aims, certainly, but almost as much in how the concept of aim is to be understood as in substantive questions of what aims should be. Where it has turned to the substantive questions, it has concentrated for the most part on particular aims, like 'happiness', 'growth', 'mental health', 'autonomy', without trying in a more global way to see how these and other aims should be interrelated and what priorities there should be among them.

Philosophers of education have often, even in these piecemeal studies, been chary of saying what they think aims ought to be because they have felt this kind of question lies outside their discipline: philosophy does not prescribe what ought to happen; its job is to clarify in a 'second-order' way the concepts, arguments and assumptions embedded in theories, in this context educational theories. And here we touch, perhaps, on the underlying reason why there has been no full-length treatment of aims. Educational theory has been parcelled up over the last twenty or thirty years into separate specialisms: psychology of education, sociology of education, history of education, philosophy of education, and so on. To none of these has been allocated the task of investigating what the aims of education should be. Sociologists might legitimately enquire what aims actually exist and seek explanations of why we have the aims we do. Other empirical workers can study the historical evolution of aims or compare them internationally. The philosophers' attitudes I have already described.

All this has been rather hard on teachers and student-teachers. Especially in an autonomous school system like the English, where schools in theory set their own aims, many students and teachers – at least those of them not implacably hostile to educational theory – would have welcomed some guidance on the topic, if only as a spur to their own thoughts about it. Philosophers of education have helped, certainly, with their piecemeal studies, but there has been next to no attempt at a global picture simply because it has been no one's job to provide it.[1] To give one example. Until the last few years the PGCE course at the London Institute, the largest of its kind in the country, included *no* general classes on what the aims of education ought to be, despite the heavily theoretical orientation of that course.

The present book tries to provide an overall picture of aims, their priorities and interrelationships. It is broadly philosophical, although if anyone should object that where I leave off 'neutral' analysis and put forward what I think our aims ought to be I am no longer doing philosophy, I would not be too alarmed. Call it what you like – casuistry, moralising, even the 'mush' from which the new-style specialisation of educational theory has allegedly rescued us – it is still better, I would submit, that there be *some* considered treatment of the topic than that it never be discussed at all. Fortunately, however, the line between philosophising and making practical recommendations is now much more blurred than it was even twenty years ago, so if I *were* worried about falling off philosophy's greasy pole into the mud – which I am not – my anxiety might be misplaced.[2]

The chapter headings on the contents page give a fair picture of how the book will proceed. Chapter 1 is introductory, discussing among other things whether we need aims at all or can make do without them. Chapter 2 looks at intrinsic aims, especially the pursuit of knowledge or understanding for its own sake. Chapter 3 takes us into pupil-centred aims and into how one is to understand the good of the pupil. Chapters 4 and 5 are really parts of one long chapter on socially oriented aims. The first relates the pupil-centred aims of chapter 3 to aims of both an economic and a moral sort. The second – chapter 5 – extends the discussion of moral aims back into the economic area and in the direction of education for citizenship. Chapter 6 pulls earlier threads together by giving an overall sketch of the educated man; and the final chapter 7 tackles the problem of how educational aims are to be realised in practice, paying particular attention to the contemporary British scene.

Chapter 1

Introduction

This book attempts to answer a single question: 'What ought to be the aims of education?' It is a question which will naturally be of interest to teachers, especially school teachers, for it is they who must structure out the details of their syllabuses and methods of teaching in the light of wider aims. But teachers, though numerous, do not form the largest category of educators in our community. Parents do. Although not all parents would see themselves in this role, treating our opening question about aims as something of interest only to professional educators, they have a duty to be concerned with it, nevertheless. For the first five years of their child's life they are often his sole educators; and their attitudes to what happens to him after this age, once he is at school, can be crucial to whether his later education is a success or a failure.

Not only teachers and parents may have a responsibility to reflect on what the aims of education should be: *every* citizen has an interest in this. 'What should our society be like?' is a question which as a citizen he cannot avoid. It overlaps so much with the question about education that the two cannot sensibly be kept apart; so although for some, for teachers and parents, the educational question is of immediate practical importance since the answer to it helps to shape even the very details of their job or role, it also has a broader relevance for all of us.

This question 'What ought to be the aims of education?' is also inextricably connected with another: 'Who ought to determine what these aims are?' 'Determine' here does not mean 'reflect on'. Anyone, presumably can do the latter. I, for instance, do it in this book; but I would not for that reason claim to determine, i.e. decide on, the aims which educational institutions like schools should adopt. And this is what is intended by the question. Any school has to have aims which help it to structure out its curricula, syllabuses and teaching methods. Who is to decide what these aims shall be? Is it, as has been recently, if not quite traditionally, so in England and Wales, the headmaster or headmistress, with or without the aid of other teachers? Or is it, as some are now coming to believe, central or local government, or perhaps a combination of teachers, politicians and parents?

The two questions, about the content and about the control of aims, cannot be discussed in isolation from each other, because answers to the one often imply answers to the other. Very broadly, there are two ways of approaching the question about what aims should be. One is to say that education proper is a more or less self-contained enterprise. Its aims are intrinsic to itself. Those who know best what these aims should be are those who know most about education, that is, teachers. The second approach questions this self-containedness. It holds that there is no good reason for separating education from the wider society. It is, indeed, a preparation for life within that society, forming its future workers and citizens. Since teachers have no special expertise in determining what the educational demands of industry should be or what citizenship should consist in, control of aims, one may hold, should pass out of their hands.

Not everyone who has reflected on aims will find himself in either one or other of these camps. Some have a foot in both, arguing that education has aims which are both intrinsic and extrinsic. My separation of the two broad approaches, useful though it is as a landmark, is too crude to do justice to the great variety of views on this topic. Not all, for instance, who would agree that education has social aims would like to see the teaching profession lose its traditional powers to determine what these should be.

To go further into these complexities would be to go into substantive argument which is better left until later. Henceforth I shall be concentrating on the question 'What ought the aims to be?', drawing out as I go the implications for the other question about who should determine them.

On the main issue, I have tried to cast my net wide enough to catch all the main opinions currently at large in the world of education. Some say that education should promote the growth of understanding (or knowledge, or reason, or the mind) for its own sake; others, that it should help each pupil to develop his potentialities to the full. Some see 'individuality' or 'personal autonomy' as of first importance. Some believe in all-round development, in a balance between intellectual and practical achievements or between the arts and the sciences; others put more emphasis on excellence within specialisms. Others again, speak of the needs of society, of ensuring a literate and numerate work-force, or an intelligent participatory democracy. Some stress art and culture, others moral character: the list of aims is almost endless. All those mentioned will be familiar to the teacher, whether as doctrines encountered in his training days or as the products of experience. I suspect, however, that relatively few teachers will have had the opportunity to sift patiently through them, weighing one aim against another, seeing how each is related to each, and coming to a reasoned conclusion about which are finally acceptable.

Unless those who work in education are clear on such things, the quality of what is provided is bound to suffer. Assuming that tradition can no longer be relied on to furnish the educational system with a set of agreed aims, cohesion between its different parts is endangered. The work of primary schools must mesh in with that of secondary schools, and the latter with that of colleges and universities. Teacher-training institutions must be in gear with what is going on in the schools. This inter-institutional co-operation requires a certain measure of agreement about objectives. If this is not to depend on custom, only rational discussion can attain it. The same is obviously true not only between institutions, but also within them. On a school staff, each person's contribution to a particular child's education must fit in with that of everyone else if the child's learning is to be a coherent whole. This, too, needs collective reflection about ends no less than means. But if this is granted, how should we set about this reflection? What guidelines should we follow in trying to settle what the aims of education should be?

A revised concept of education

It may seem obvious to some that one cannot say what the aims of education should be until one has worked out what education itself is. Some analytically inclined philosophers of education have been particularly attracted to this argument in recent years. They have seen their central task as the 'analysis' of the concept of education: once we are clear with what other ideas the idea of education is logically connected, they suppose, we can then go on to ask questions about its aims or justification. We might, indeed, see that these questions have already been answered, or partly answered, by the analysis itself. To understand the aims that footballers have in playing football we have to understand what football is. Once we understand that, we see that it has certain aims intrinsic to itself (e.g. that each team should score more goals than its opponent), quite apart from any extrinsic aims the players might have, like celebrity or wealth. Is it not likely that education is like football in this respect? By discovering by logical analysis what the enterprise essentially involves, can we not discover at least its intrinsic aims?

This has been the hope of several educational philosophers over the past two decades. But the hope has not been realised. The difficulty has been that, whereas it is not at all hard to give a neutral account of what football is which everyone can accept, few 'analyses' of education so far produced have been uncontested. The analysers have generally been charged with writing their own accounts of what education *ought to be* into their descriptions of what the concept involves. If intrinsic aims of education emerge at the end of their analysis, these are only those value-judgments which they fed in from the start.

Feeding in these aims or value-judgments is no bad thing in itself. A large part of the present book, in fact, will revolve around such value-judgments. The drawback in including them in one's analyses is that they are often left unargued-for. If one *did* begin to argue for them, showing the grounds on which they rested, their relations with other aims, their superiority to rejected candidates, and so on, one would soon see that this was a major study in its own right, see, that is, that one could not succeed in one's plan of discovering what education is before an exhaustive discussion of what its aims should be.

Failure to engage in this, born of over-eagerness to get on with the 'analysis', can have unfortunate consequences, including practical ones. Take, for instance, the account of education in *Education and Personal Relationships* by R. Downie, E. Loudfoot and E. Telfer. These authors rightly reject an older attempt to give something like a definition of 'education' as 'initiation into intrinsically worthwhile activities', arguing that this writes out the possibility of extrinsic aims from the start: it rests on the value-judgment that education ought to be concerned only with activities valuable for their own sake. They go on to state that they are going to give a 'neutral' account of education which allows the possibility of both intrinsic and extrinsic aims. This is that the educated man is one who possesses a broad range of knowledge of different types – knowledge of facts, practical knowledge of how to do things, knowledge by acquaintance with works of art and other objects. Their more detailed specification of their concept does not concern us here: we need only note their claim that their description of it tallies with what those who work in educational institutions by and large take education to be. Having sketched out their concept, they then turn to its justification. Why should knowledge, as specified, be the hallmark of the educated man? There are, they argue, two kinds of reasons: intrinsic ones (i.e. that knowledge is desirable in itself) and extrinsic ones (i.e. that knowledge is necessary or desirable for further ends, like individual happiness, moral character or the good of society). Not all these reasons are necessarily acceptable; Downie *et al.* spend a large part of their book winnowing away those which are not.

In tying educatedness so closely to the possession of knowledge, these authors run the danger of unduly restricting its scope. Many would argue that educating children is as much a matter of shaping character as of imparting knowledge: knowledge can be used for good or evil purposes, so educators have to build up such dispositions to act morally that the latter is unthinkable. I am not, by the way, necessarily *advocating* this idea of education. The point is, rather, a methodological one. If one begins by delineating the concept of education, one runs the risk of overlooking a whole dimension of possible aims at the outset. And when one then turns, as Downie *et al.* do, to discuss justifications, the scope of what is being justified is already circumscribed: reasons why the educated man should be a knower may be discussed in full; but whether, for instance, he should be of a benevolent or self-centred disposition may never come into question.

'Still', some might say, 'even if Downie's, or others', accounts of education won't do, if we're asking what the aims of education ought to be, we've got to know what we're talking about. So we've got to have *some* understanding of what education is.'

Very well. Suppose I try to describe it in as vanilla-flavoured a way as possible. Let me stipulate that education is simply upbringing. In asking what the aims of education ought to be, I shall be taking this to mean: what should we aim at in bringing up children or young people? What kinds of achievements, of character, intellect or whatever, should we wish them to possess? I hope that my formulation of the question in this way is wide-meshed enough to include as broad a range of putative aims as possible and not close off any options. Objectors may want to pick a bone over the term 'upbringing', some arguing that it is broader in application than education, others, bearing such things as adult education in mind, that it is narrower. But I have lost whatever passion I may have had in the past for conceptual joustings of this kind. At an opposite pole from those who cannot stay to examine their implicit beliefs about aims in their haste to worry away at their concepts, I am anxious – some might say *too* anxious – to leave concept analysis behind me and proceed to my main business as soon as possible. The people most puzzled about the aims of education because this has practical consequences for their work or their lives more generally – the teachers, the parents, the citizens – are concerned above all with how children should be brought up. So am I. If there are others of a more purely theoretical and specifically of a more lexicographical, turn of mind, I shall have to leave them at this point to their own preoccupations.

Are aims necessary?

So I shall reject the way into our subject via the analysis of concepts. Instead, I shall go directly to the various answers that have been given to the question about aims. But before we begin, it will be as well to clear one thing out of the way. From the start of the next chapter and throughout the rest of the book I shall be taking it for granted that education should be aimed at *something*, even though there are disputes about what that something should be. It may seem self-evident that educators need aims. Educating is surely an intentional, purposeful enterprise – how could it be otherwise? Yet the question has been raised in recent years 'Must an educator have an aim?' (Peters, 1959); and the answers which some have given seem to challenge this apparent self-evidentness.

None of these answers, however, succeeds in undermining it. Some have objected to aims like growth, or happiness, or the good of society, because they are so general as to be useless as practical guides. In their place some would put more limited and attainable 'objectives', often of a 'behavioural' sort – e.g. that pupils following such and such a course in French should be able to use such and such grammatical constructions at the end of it. Others would place less emphasis on aims than on 'principles of procedure'. Among the most important things that a teacher teaches are, for instance, a respect for rationality, benevolence and tolerance; but these are not written down in syllabuses but enshrined in the very manner in which he conducts his classes. In fixing our gaze on end-products, it is argued, we can very easily overlook the ethical quality of the means adopted.

Neither of these positions destroys the case for aims. Aims cannot be replaced by objectives, since objectives, even though they may be small-scale, are still aims. More than this, small-scale objectives, like the ability to use certain verb-forms in French, surely need some kind of rationale if they are not to be wholly arbitrary; and it is hard to see how this further justification, if we press it back far enough, can avoid referring to more general aims.

As for the emphasis on principles of procedure, this takes it for granted that the teacher wants to instil in his pupils a respect for rationality, benevolence, or whatever. In so far as he does, this is what he is aiming at. The fact that he tries to bring about this aim not by textbook instruction but by a certain manner of teaching does nothing to show that he has no aims, or that aims are less important than people have sometimes thought.

There is more to be said about both these critical points of view. They remind us both that it is not enough to have more general aims, since more specific objectives are necessary, too; and that these more general aims cannot always be specified in curriculum objectives but are sometimes realised in principles of procedure. On the 'objectives' approach, there is more, too, to be said about the claim that only 'behavioural' objectives are satisfactory. But since the conceptual confusions surrounding this claim have been adequately discussed in recent years, I shall say no more about them here.

I have still not fully dealt with the claim that high-level statements of aim are useless as practical guides to action. The first page of Sir Percy Nunn's *Education* provides perhaps its most celebrated and influential expression. Nunn believes that the attempt to state a universal aim for education is largely misconceived, since people's interpretation of whatever aim is proposed will differ according to their different ideals of life: what counts as the 'formation of character' or a 'preparation for complete living' for A will be 'ridiculous or rankly offensive' to B, and so on. 'A cynic might declare', he tells us, 'that the real use of the maxims we have quoted is to conceal, as behind a verbal fog-screen, differences of educational faith and practice too radical to be harmonised and too serious to be exposed to the public view' (Nunn, 1920, p. 9).

What alternative does Nunn put forward? He holds very firmly to the view that ideals of life vary considerably between individuals. 'It follows that there can be no universal aim of education if that aim is to include the assertion of any particular ideal of life; for there are as many ideals as there are persons' (p. 13). Instead, 'educational efforts must, it would seem, be limited to securing for every one the conditions under which his individuality is most completely developed' (*ibid.*).

Nunn's argument here is a muddle. He has not shown what he set out to show, that there can be no universal aim of education. For to insist on the complete development of individuality is surely to demand a universal aim. Nunn states that universal aims are impossible if they embody any particular ideal of life. But his own advocacy of individuality embodies one such ideal. Not everyone would share it, least of all in the biologically oriented interpretation he later gives it (and which we shall be discussing in chapter 3). Like any other universal aim, it stands in need of justification.

Nunn's confusion on this point has persisted into our generation, partly owing to the long-lasting popularity of his book. Many of those in the 'child-centred' tradition, which Nunn did so much to promote, will tell you that it is wrong for a teacher to impose aims on children, since if the latter are to develop to the full, they must be allowed to discover and try to realise their own aims for themselves. The covert aim here is as often as not unrecognised.

I hope these considerations are enough to rebut the claim that aims are unimportant. Henceforth I shall be taking it that they are essential and that the most urgent task is to see which aims are most acceptable. But before we leave the anti-aims position, there is just one more thing to be said about it. I stated earlier that the question 'What should the aims of education be?' is not independent of the question 'Who should determine aims?' Our recent discussion shows us one way in which this is so. If aims are not to be imposed on children, *a fortiori* aims are not to be imposed by those outside the school, whether local authorities, central government, the Schools Council, or any other body. Teachers holding this view are likely, therefore, to resist current pressures to remove the autonomy of the schools in matters of aims and curricula.

They are not alone in this. In the next chapter we will meet another group of educationists who support the schools' autonomy for rather different reasons.

Chapter 2

Intrinsic aims

It is hard to give an accurate account of the thesis that education should have 'intrinsic' aims without bringing in all sorts of distinctions and qualifications, but the main thrust of the argument should be clear enough. It is that educational achievements – the knowledge and skills, for instance, which children come to possess – should be seen as valuable for their own sake, quite apart from any other value they may have, of a vocational kind, for instance.

Many teachers and educationists will assent to this 'intrinsic' theory. No doubt there will be differences of emphasis. Some may want to claim that the *only* educational aims are intrinsic; others, perhaps a larger number, that while other, e.g. vocational or social, aims are not to be neglected, intrinsic aims are of great, even of central, importance. There may also be differences in the kinds of educational achievements. Some will hold that it is *knowledge*, in some form or other, that is important for its own sake; while others will include other things, too, like aesthetic appreciation or creativeness, and perhaps more besides. Among those who stress the importance of knowledge, there is, finally, a further distinction to be made between those who say that the mere *possession* of knowledge is intrinsically valuable and those who predicate this not of its possession, but of its *pursuit*: the latter would argue that the aim of teaching history, for instance, should not be that pupils acquire a body of historical knowledge or skills of enquiry, but that they become actively involved in historical research.

Types of justification

It would be tedious to go into all these variations on the same theme. It is the theme itself we need to examine, especially the justifications which might be offered for it. The crucial question is: why should some at least of the aims of education be intrinsic?

We touched on one answer in the last chapter. 'Education' could be so defined – as 'initiation into intrinsically worthwhile activities', for instance – that it is analytically true that it must have intrinsic aims. But clearly such a move would not get us very far, since we would still need to know whether we should adopt this definition of education or reject it – which is tantamount to wondering what we were wondering in the first place, i.e. whether aims should or should not be intrinsic.

A more substantial answer, popular among philosophers of education in the later 1960s, rests on a so-called 'transcendental' argument (Peters, 1966 p. 164; Hirst, 1965, p. 126). This argument has been thoroughly discussed and criticised elsewhere and my strong impression is that few, if any, of its original proponents would still wish to adhere to it (see White, 1973, ch. 2; Downie *et al.*, 1974, ch. 3). The argument is at its most plausible when used to justify the particular claim that the pursuit of *knowledge* is intrinsically worthwhile. It asserts that if anyone either doubts or denies this claim, he can be brought to see, assuming he is a rational person, that there is an ineradicable inconsistency in his position. For in asking 'why pursue knowledge?', the sceptic is in fact already committed to the pursuit of what he is seeking to justify: it is presupposed to his seriously asking the question that he thinks it worthwhile to try to arrive at a well-grounded, true belief about the topic in question, i.e. to come to know something. Seductive though the argument may be at first sight, it is pretty clearly inadequate on closer inspection. For the sceptic is not 'committed to the pursuit of knowledge' in the sense that educationists have in mind, that is, to the pursuit of some or other *branch* of knowledge, like history or science, still less to the pursuit of all branches of it without distinction: the most he is committed to seeking is the specific piece of knowledge which answers his question. *Any* questioner is committed to the pursuit of knowledge in this very attenuated sense – the man who asks 'What's the time?', for instance, wants to know what the time is – but he is not *ipso facto* committed to the pursuit of history, mathematics or whatever.

There are all sorts of other difficulties with this kind of 'transcendental' justification: it does not show, for instance, why knowledge is to be sought *for its own sake*, since there is no guarantee that the questioner has not extrinsic reasons for asking his question; and even if we assume its conclusion, that knowledge is intrinsically valuable, we still have been given no reason why *education* must have this aim (without, that is, making this true by definition). But there is no need to rake over these dead leaves again.

A third way of justifying the 'intrinsic' thesis is found in the book by Downie *et al.*, *Education and Personal Relationships* (1974) already mentioned. Being educated, in their view, is possessing a broad range of different types of knowledge and understanding. Rejecting the 'transcendental' justification, they go on to say:

> The simplest justification for education which can be offered – and perhaps the one which in the final showing is the most satisfactory – is that its intrinsic aims, those states of mind which constitute it, are good in themselves or desirable for their own sakes. If it be asked how we can know this the reply is that many people, in every age, have claimed it to be so – in other words our appeal is to what would now be called intuition. Of course, the details of the content would vary from age to age but the general idea – that a cultivated mind, or the possession of knowledge and understanding, are goods in themselves – is a very widespread one with a long history. Whether we can strictly speak of *knowledge* based on such an intuition is, however, rather doubtful, since there seem to be no ways of checking or verifying it; we should speak instead of 'faith' or 'conviction' (p. 50).

This argument for intrinsic aims is no more persuasive than its two predecessors, although in one way it is more illuminating. It tells us that many people in every age have held the conviction that the possession of knowledge is good in itself. But that fact does nothing to show that knowledge-possession *is* good in itself: all these people may have been wrong. Downie *et al.* say a little later that it is 'implausible to suppose' that this widespread belief 'is entirely based on illusion' (p. 52); they do not, however, say *why* it is implausible.

Though not convincing, the argument's reminder that, historically, the intrinsic theory has always been popular helps us to see it in perspective. Fifty to a hundred years ago there would have been no problem of justifying the possession or pursuit of knowledge for its own sake as a fundamental aim. That was a period in which the foundations of our present system of state education were being laid: beliefs about education were built into the growing structure at that time and are often still with us, perhaps in attenuated forms. The dominant philosophy in Britain during that period was a version of Hegelian idealism deriving from T. H. Green and 𝐅. H. Bradley. Green, especially, had both personally and via his disciples a lasting influence on the shaping of our national education system and the ideas which pervaded it (Gordon and White, 1979).

In his *Prolegomena to Ethics* Green sets forth, implicitly, a philosophy of education. It is a religious philosophy. God, as in Hegel, is conceived of as Thought or Reason. The world we live in, ourselves included, is animated by a divine purpose: in it God is progressively coming to realise Himself, a process only complete when He becomes fully conscious of his own being as Thought. How, though, is God to achieve this self-realisation? He is not, as in other doctrines, a transcendent creator of the universe: the universe is itself the expression of an immanent divinity. Inanimate nature cannot provide the self-consciousness required. It is only in man that this is found. Men are thus vehicles of God: it is only as they grow both in self-understanding and in understanding of the natural world that God can come to know Himself. The highest aim of human life, therefore, is to participate in this divine self-realisation. His end is also ours. We collectively achieve self-realisation as we grow towards higher and higher levels of consciousness, becoming more knowledgeable, more rational, with a wider understanding of ourselves and of the world. It is not important in this theory that the knowledge or understanding be applied to anything outside itself, to the solution of technological problems, for instance: God is pure thought, and as men grow in pure thought, they become His vehicles.

In idealism, therefore, the educational aim of fostering the growth of knowledge for its own sake could be justified by reference to a wider metaphysics. There would have been no problem for philosophically inclined educationists around the turn of the century in showing why this aim should be pursued: to them, given their religious assumptions, its desirability must have seemed self-evident.

Hegelian idealism owed much to Aristotle. Aristotle, too, held that education should aim at knowledge for its own sake. He, too, grounded this on the belief that man's purpose is predetermined for him: it is to live that kind of life for which he is most fitted by nature. Since it is the possession of reason which distinguishes man from lower animals, man's end, and the end of his education, is to pursue rational activities, for no other reason than that they are rational.

Knowledge for its own sake has been a hallowed educational aim, then, since the Greeks. The metaphysical web with which Aristotle surrounded it was thickened, perhaps made more opaque, but perhaps not strengthened, by nineteenth-century thought, not least idealism. This is not the place for a critical discussion of these older versions of the intrinsic thesis, though they obviously depend on assumptions which make them difficult for many to accept today, not least their common teleological assumption that human ends are predetermined, by nature or by God. The main reason for mentioning these older versions is the light they throw, by contrast, on the status of intrinsic thesis today. It still persists in many quarters, but is denuded now of its old clothing: it stands detached, self-subsistent, disconnected from wider considerations.

This disconnection did not happen overnight. An important intermediary between the theory as it was in the hands of the idealists and the sparser theory it is today was John Dewey.

Dewey was bowled over as a young man by the idealism of T. H. Green. Like many religious men of his day, Dewey found himself in a spiritual confusion, increasingly unable to square non-conformist doctrines with new scientific ideas, not least those of Darwin. Green's rationalistic version of religion seemed to bypass worries about evolution and historical examinations of the Bible. Hence its great appeal. In proceeding further along a rationalist path, Dewey quickly came to lose his religious faith entirely and therewith his commitment to idealist philosophy. But he retained a number of its features in his own work. First, as with the idealists, philosophy for him remained closely tied to educational ends: it never became a hived-off end in itself. He kept, too, the basic idealist concept of self-realisation, although he early changed his terminology and came to speak of it as 'growth'. Again, just as the fundamental aim of education for the idealists was the unending raising of the individual's consciousness to fit it more and more as a vehicle of divine spirit, so, too, in Dewey, education is essentially to do with promoting the growth of the individual mind without limit. Education for him has no aims outside itself: growth is an intrinsic aim (Dewey, 1916, p. 50). The idealists, too, might well have said the same. But for them there was a metaphysical rationale which is lacking in Dewey, or transposed into a different key. Raising men's consciousness was not, to the idealist, a means of promoting an *extrinsic* aim, namely, the furtherance of God's purposes: God only existed as reason, so the apparently extrinsic aim was, after all, intrinsic. Dewey lopped away the religious rationale, leaving only growth for its own sake. Or, rather, since nature in evolution came to replace, for Dewey, the gradual unfolding of a divine purpose in the world, growth was important, in the final analysis, because it was in line with the openendedness of evolutionary progress.

Dewey's shift from a religious to a biological perspective also brought with it a change in his conception of 'growth' itself. For the idealists, mental development was ratiocinative and contemplative. For Dewey, impressed by the evolution of mind in nature, it became above all practical, taking the form of adapting new means to ends when usual means were unavailable. Intelligence was reconceptualised as problem solving.

In retaining the thesis that education has no ends beyond the growth of consciousness for its own sake, while at the same time emptying it of its old religious rationale, Dewey helped to ensure its continuance into our own times.

Has knowledge for its own sake *no* place, then, in a secular society like our own? Even if its old metaphysical rationale is gone, is it true that nothing can replace it?

Alasdair MacIntyre (1964) has proposed a non-religious argument for it which many will find congenial. In his article 'Against Utilitarianism', MacIntyre argues that education should not aim only at instrumental goods – access to jobs, increased industrial production, increased consumption of goods and services, which in turn keeps up production, and so on. A society which pursues only means, without paying attention to any ultimate ends which these means might bring about, is irrational. So, too, is an educational system. The aim of education, according to MacIntyre,

> ought to be to help people to discover activities whose ends are not
> outside themselves; and it happens to be of the nature of all
> intellectual enquiry that in and for itself it provides just such activity.
> The critical ability which ought to be the fruit of education serves
> nothing directly except for itself, no one except those who exercise it
> (p. 19).

A page or so later MacIntyre clarifies this a little further. Rational, critical enquiry is not to be restricted narrowly to theoretical activities. 'Unless the feelings too are sifted and criticized, the feelings are simply handed over to unreason' (p. 21). Art, we may suppose, as well as science or philosophy, is to find its place among things of final value. Not only these. The aim is more general. 'Above all the task of education is to teach the value of activity done for its own sake' (*ibid.*).

MacIntyre's line of thought finds echoes in other writers. He, however, like many of them, fails to make a quite crucial distinction. There are, in fact, two very different theories of education entwined together in his account. One is valid and of the first importance, although rarely given due weight in actual educational arrangements. The second is invalid but fits in well with conventional assumptions.

The first theory is that education should not only be concerned with means to ends, but must do something to promote ends themselves. This is surely acceptable: there *would* be something irrational if educators only concentrated on means to further means to further means. ... Now this first theory does not imply that education should not be concerned with means at all, only that it is not enough for it to be so concerned. Neither, more importantly, does it imply that in paying attention to ends, these should be only the *pupil*'s ends. One might hold that pupils should be brought up to believe that they should help *others* as well as themselves to engage in activities done for their own sake. This would be fully compatible with this first theory.

The second theory is that education should aim at the *pupil*'s engagement in (critical) activity for its own sake. 'The critical ability which ought to be the fruit of education serves nothing directly except for itself, no one except those who exercise it' (p. 19). This second theory is unfounded, as was implied in the last paragraph. The pupil-centred conclusion may *seem* to follow from the proposition, mentioned above, that education should promote involvement in ends-in-themselves. But it does not in fact follow.

The distinction between the two theories is by no means pedantic. It is of the highest importance, since it separates two entirely different conceptions of education. Take, for instance, a secondary school which runs a course on technology, not as an end-in-itself but as a contribution to creating a society where all, not merely some, are involved in some way in ultimate ends. On the second view, the school would be deviating from the proper ends of education, since it is not concerned exclusively with the *pupil*'s ultimate ends; on the first, which says only that education should be concerned with ends, not necessarily the pupil's, the school would not be deviating.

It is only the first, not the second, theory, which can be rationally justified. But in concession to the second theory one must agree that if it is 'everyone' who is to engage in ends-in-themselves – and this has not yet been shown – the pupil himself must be included. And for him so to engage, it might be argued, he must have some understanding, and perhaps some experience, of this engagement. His education could not consist *solely* in instrumental activities, however much these were subservient to humane and reasonable ends. If they were, he might well be cut off from engaging in these ends himself. And if we universalised this latter thought so as to include everyone, we could be back with a society where everyone is preoccupied with means and no one is able to engage in anything as an end.

Although MacIntyre argues for a specific sort of end-in-itself as the educator's aim, namely intellectual enquiry, in neither of the two forms just outlined does his theory show why this *specific* end should be highlighted. For the theory only shows that it is a condition of rational behaviour that there be ends-in-themselves. It has not given any content, as yet, to these ends. In particular, it has not identified them with intellectual pursuits. It emphasises only the *intrinsic* nature of these ends; dancing and tennis, pursued for their own sakes, could, *as far as this argument goes*, be among them.

The theory that the aim, or the central aim, of education should be that the pupil possess or pursue knowledge or understanding for its own sake remains ungrounded, except by religious or metaphysical doctrines which many today find less plausible than their predecessors did in the last century. If all the arguments in its favour are rejected, will any others do better? If not, then many pupils in our schools and universities are being seriously misled. They are being encouraged to work away at medieval history or higher mathematics not for any extrinsic reason – to promote their own well-being or that of the community – but for. ... For what? If we say 'for intrinsic reasons', then what are these reasons? We still have not been given any. As someone who did indeed work in this way in my youth, I speak with some passion. In my sixth form I studied medieval history. Although there were always extrinsic incentives, I felt that I should ideally ignore these and do the subject 'for its own sake'. What this 'for its own sake' meant was never clear to me, but I assumed that the fault lay in my own ignorance: the more I plunged into the heart of medieval studies, the more I should find the answer there. That there was a reason I never doubted. At university I read history and concentrated even more microscopically on the Middle Ages. But I never found the answer I was looking for and owing to an unquestioning acceptance of what my schoolmasters taught me to believe about the ends of education, I finished my long and expensive education with a fair knowledge of the life of St Bernard and an almost absolute ignorance of anything else. Many others, I am sure, could tell a similar tale. The moral for any schoolteacher should be clear: do think through your unexamined views about the ends of education – years of your pupils' lives may be blighted if your aims are ill-conceived and if they take those aims all too seriously.

Mention of the *pupil*'s reasons for studying a curriculum subject reminds us that the main purpose of this book is to sort out what the *educator*'s aims should be and that his aims may well sometimes be different from the pupil's. In the case I cited, I as a pupil had taken over the aims, or what I believed to be the aims, of my teachers. But often, of course, the educator's aims are not all obvious to the pupil, especially the younger pupil. A primary-school teacher may be teaching arithmetic by dividing her class up into a number of shops, each with its assistants and customers. For the children, this is little more than a game, enjoyable for its own sake; for the teacher, perhaps, it is a step on the road to a basic vocational education or to the formation of good citizens. One can hold either of the latter aims, which are far from 'intrinsic', and at the same time believe that children should at least sometimes be absorbed in classroom activities for their own sake. Those who argue that education should be about knowledge for its own sake may have this pupil perspective in mind: learning should not be for the sake of extrinsic rewards – positions in class, prizes, teacher's approval – but for its own sake. I do not want to go into the pros and cons of this thesis here. All I want to do is to make plain that it is different from the similarly named 'intrinsic' thesis about the aims of education. I stress the difference because it is easy to conflate the two – to begin, for instance, from the not at all implausible claim that children, when learning, should enjoy doing so for its own sake, and then move without noticing it to the quite different claim that the ultimate educational reason for learning anything is that it be enjoyed for its own sake.

Excellence and selection

The centrality among aims of knowledge – or more broadly intellectual and aesthetic activity – for its own sake deserves to be challenged. It is firmly entrenched in elitist educational institutions, whether maintained grammar or independent schools. This is not in itself a reason against it: I would not wish to be thought guilty of the bad argument 'the grammar (or public) school has this aim, therefore it won't do.' The reasons why it should be challenged have, in any case, been adequately exposed already. But as a matter of empirical fact the aims which selective schools have set before themselves have tended to be taken over by other schools (e.g. many secondary moderns and comprehensives) in a watered-down form, so that knowledge-for-its-own-sake has come to permeate, to different degrees in different institutions, the whole educational system. It is by no means unchallenged, especially these days, but, even so, its standing, among schoolteachers and the public alike, has been and remains high.

If the centrality of this aim is *not* justified, therefore, the education of many millions of children is still, as it has been for many years, on the wrong lines.

Supporters of a selective (including an independent) system have often held that the aim is, in any case, suited only to the education of the minority and should not be extended to every pupil. On what grounds?

Sometimes the idea, often left unformulated, has been that the pursuit of intellectual and aesthetic activities for their own sake only makes sense for those with leisure. The leisure class has traditionally been the aristocracy, broadened especially in the nineteenth century to include the richer elements among the middle classes. The public-school education which upper-class children have received has been founded partly on the Aristotelian idea that a leisure class should be differently educated from the rest of the population. Those without leisure – Aristotle's slaves, the modern proletariate – should learn what is necessary to keep the class-divided society in being, i.e. instrumental skills rather than things of intrinsic value.

Another justification, not necessarily tied to a class system, has been in terms of excellence. Given a society that prizes excellence in intellectual and artistic pursuits of an intrinsic sort, and given that scholars and artists are more likely to achieve excellence if they have been taught in high-powered schools devoted to these values, and given that the majority of pupils lack the ability to profit by attendance at such schools, the society in question has good reason to set up a selective system where the minority of gifted pupils work towards the intrinsic aims in selective schools while the majority work towards others elsewhere (Cooper, 1980, chs 2 and 3).

This second justification differs from the first in two important ways. It is not interested in the preservation of a hereditary upper class but in a meritocracy where admission to the group of creative individuals is open to everyone of high ability. And whereas the hereditary upper class of the first argument engages in cultural activities in its leisure time, there is no thought that it should achieve *excellence* in these areas: many of its members, for one thing, will lack the ability to do so.

How acceptable are these justifications?

The first rests on the assumption that a permanent leisure class should be preserved. What grounds could there be for this? If it is argued that such a class is necessary to provide excellence in intellectual and artistic pursuits, this clearly rests on the second justification, which we shall come to in a moment. But it would also have to be shown why a *permanent* leisure class rather than a meritocratic one is necessary. I know of nothing in support of this. It also fails to show why the children of this class should be educated with a view to achieving knowledge (etc.) for its own sake. If no good reasons can be found to support the aim in general, then no good reasons can support it when restricted to one social class. It follows that many public-school children who are currently being brought up to believe in the overriding importance of this aim may be being seriously misled.

The second justification states that education, for some pupils only, ought to be directed towards the promotion of excellence in intellectual and aesthetic activities of an intrinsic sort. But why so? As well as the familiar problem of justifying the pursuit of knowledge (etc.) for its own sake, it also faces the question: why *excellence*? Pupils are to be stretched to the limits so that they produce work of as high a quality as possible. To some people this may seem self-evidently desirable. But it is not so in fact. Suppose a child shows some aptitude for mathematics and is driven on, or encouraged, by his teachers to achieve university-level work, say, by the age of 14. Is this necessarily a good thing? Is it necessarily good *for him*? National schools of ballet often select talented children at an early age; as well as giving them a general education, they teach them to perform at very high levels of achievement. Ex-pupils sometimes complain that they were steered into a particular channel at too early an age, before they were in a position to decide what sort of life they wanted to lead. The same complaints are heard from those in other schools who have undergone intensive courses of a more theoretical sort. Of course, these people may be misguided in their belief that their high-powered schooling did not benefit them. We will be in a position to say more about this when we have examined the topic of the pupil's good in the next chapter. Meanwhile the onus is on the defender of 'excellence' to show, if this is his thesis, that the sort of education he favours is indeed in the interests of the pupil. Prima facie, it does not look as if it always is.

But he might seek to justify excellence on other grounds. Percy Nunn (1920) believed in selective education for a creative elite because this was in line with evolutionary progress as he saw it. This view assumes a teleological theory of evolution: men have to understand nature's purposes and organise their education systems so that they work with nature and not against her. Not everyone would be willing these days to accept such a teleology.

Percy Nunn held that the good of the individual pupil coincides with the good of the human species as a whole; so there is no danger, in his theory, that education for intrinsic intellectual aims *sacrifices* the pupil for the sake of something else. But other justifications might risk this. The emphasis might be put on academic disciplines as institutions. The important thing is now that the discipline of science (etc.) is in a flourishing state: promising pupils are sent to high-powered schools which will turn them out as devoted servants of the disciplines. On this interpretation, there *is*, prima facie, a possible clash with the well-being of the pupil, for the reason already mentioned. It is hard to see why the interests of the academic disciplines (and artistic institutions) should be thought of overriding importance, outweighing considerations of individual well-being. (Some would say that, in the light of the influence British universities have on secondary-school curricula and examinations, the interests of academic disciplines do affect the schools' aims in exactly this way.)

I have not commented on the assumption embedded in the excellence argument, that only a few are capable of an education on these lines. Is this true? If one pitches the requirements of educational success very high indeed, so that we are talking only of the most highly creative scientists, artists and scholars, then it is reasonable to assume that their numbers will be limited. But, for this reason, few of those who go to selective schools are likely to be among them. If this is so, then there is surely something irrational in setting up a selective system in which one can comfortably predict that most will fail. But the more the criteria of educatedness are reduced — so that we are no longer talking of the Mozarts and Matisses of the first division, but of good solid academics, worthy holders, for instance, of university posts — the less obvious it becomes that only few could attain them. It has been an orthodoxy within psychology that the intellectual ceilings of most people are set so low, by genetic or other factors, that they would never be capable of work of this sort. Something like this is necessary as a rational basis of the kind of selective system now being examined. But there is no evidence, to my knowledge, in its favour; and it should not even be assumed that people *have* intellectual ceilings: it is hard, indeed, to see what general proof (or disproof) of this claim there could be (White, 1974).

These, then, are some of the difficulties in justifying the 'excellence' aim. One attempt to rescue it is not open to us in this chapter. In a recent article in *The Times* (14 July 1980), the views of Michael McCrum, the outgoing head of Eton, are reported as follows:

> To some extent the growing stress at independent schools on academic excellence had been a direct response to parental desires: better exam results, staff-pupil ratios and so on had been shown to be what they wanted, which was quite a shift from the godliness and good learning sought in the nineteenth century. If parents wanted places at Oxford and Cambridge for their children, the public schools would do their best to provide them.

Pupils, their teachers and parents can, and often do, have extrinsic reasons of a vocational sort for insisting on intrinsic aims. Here, however, I shall ignore this complication, since the new justification takes us away from purely intrinsic reasons and hence beyond the remit of the present chapter. (On the vocational aims of 'elite' education, see chapter 5.)[1]

Conclusion

I mentioned in the last chapter Downie *et al.*'s distinction between intrinsic and extrinsic justifications of education. The former seek to show why knowledge is important for its own sake, the latter why it is important for other reasons, like the good of the pupil or of society.

The discussion in this chapter has failed to reveal any reason why knowledge (etc.) for its own sake should be the central aim of education. But it has not entirely closed the door to some such aim, if not as central. Our examination of MacIntyre's account led us to see a reason why a pupil's education might aim to some extent at involving him in ends-in-themselves. We shall be looking later at what this 'involvement' might entail. Meanwhile it is at least clear that we have no reason as yet to exclude from it coming to know or understand things. Something like the 'intrinsic' aim, in other words, may be still on the cards, at least as one aim among many. But if it *is*, then Downie's way of making the distinction between intrinsic and extrinsic justifications may well have to go. It will have to go if the reasons why pupils should know things for their own sake refer to their own good or to the good of others.

If the 'intrinsic' thesis is justified in this way by reasons outside itself like the well-being of the individual or of society, then the thesis cannot be treated as a self-contained, somehow self-justifying phenomenon. Some further web of argument must lie around it: we may or may not be able to dispense with an Aristotelian or Hegelian web, but some web there must be. The point is worth making since it bears, again, on the question 'Who should determine aims?' as well as on 'What should the aims be?' If one believes that the 'intrinsic' thesis is self-contained or self-justifying, then one has every reason for resisting attempts from those outside the education system to say what its aims should be: there is nothing outside academic pursuits to which appeal can be made, and academics know best about academic pursuits. But if a full justification must refer to such things as the good of the pupil or the good of society, it is far less clear why teachers, or educators generally, should be thought to have any special authority to pronounce on such matters. If the good of society comes into the account, this seems to bring in political considerations: the question 'What should the aims of education be?' seems to become a political question, to be decided in a democracy, by the political community at large. Whether the good of society *must* come in is a topic we shall be pursuing in later chapters. But even if the 'intrinsic' thesis were backed only by reference to the pupil's own good, it would still not be clear that educators are in any privileged position over the rest of the community to say what this good is. Some of them will want to claim that they *are* so privileged. If they are, the question who should decide on aims will be answered in their favour. The question is still an open one. In the next chapter I shall be examining, among other things, the basis of this common claim that teachers and parents know what is best for their children.

Chapter 3

The good of the pupil

Introduction

More widespread, perhaps, than the view that education should aim at knowledge for its own sake, is the belief that it should promote the well-being of those who undergo it. Some, indeed, of those who hold the 'intrinsic' theory might well justify it, as suggested in the last chapter, in terms of the pupil's good. But one does not need to believe in the value of knowledge for its own sake to believe that education should be predominantly pupil-orientated. Many parents, teachers and educational theorists share this common assumption. True, there are few among them who would put *all* the emphasis on the good of the pupil. After all, there are also other people's interests to be considered: moral education is important and so is the contribution which education can make to general economic prosperity. People differ in the weight they attach to these various and sometimes conflicting considerations. But by and large what is noteworthy, at least about the contemporary English educational scene, is the convergence of opinion among those most directly involved in education that its *main* preoccupation should be with the good of the pupil.

Parents, for instance, typically think of education in this way. What they see their children's good *as*, however, is not always the same. Some tend to see it narrowly in terms of getting a 'good job', for reasons of social status or because of the opportunities that this will bring to lead a happier or more comfortable life, or for both kinds of reason. Other parents may be less interested in job prospects than in their child's being equipped to live life to the full or to make the most of his talents. Mixed motives are also, of course, very common. When a pupil's parents help him to make up his mind, for instance, about what range of subjects he will specialise in in the later years of the secondary school, reasons of all these kinds can and do come into the reckoning.

23

Teachers, too, see their work very largely in pupil-centred terms. Secondary-school work, especially after the first couple of years, is increasingly dominated by the GCE and CSE exams and although many teachers resent these external pressures on their work, they do what they can to help their pupils get as many passes and as good grades as possible, because they know what this will mean to them in job-prospects and life-chances. In this they see eye to eye with parents, but this is not to say that teachers will give the same weighting as parents to the different kinds of goals – of status, of comfort, of self-fulfilment – that examination success can help one to attain.

As for primary teachers, there is evidence from a recent survey of their aims that they, too, put pupil-orientated considerations first (Ashton *et al.*, 1975). The three most popular aims were found to be:

1   children should be happy, cheerful and well-balanced,
2   they should enjoy school work and find satisfaction in their achievements,
3   individuals should be encouraged to develop in their own ways.

All these aims have to do with the good of the pupils. Remarkably, there is a clearcut division between these first three aims and aims 4–6:

4   moral values should be taught as a basis of behaviour,
5   children should be taught to respect property,
6   they should be taught courtesy and good manners.

The latter three are other-centred, rather than pupil-centred aims. Once again, taking in the survey as a whole, then, the pupil's good takes pride of place. Once again, too, there may well be different interpretations of what this good consists in. What do the teachers mean when they say they want children to be 'happy'? Do they mean happiness *now*, as pupils, or happiness as adults? What is happiness, anyway? And what does it mean to be 'well-balanced' or to 'develop in one's own way'? How far do primary teachers' conceptions of the good of the pupil coincide with or diverge from the views of parents and secondary teachers on the same topic? Before we can reach a satisfactory conclusion on the place of pupil-centred aims in education we will clearly have to get to grips with these questions.

And not only with these. Educational theorists, as well as parents and teachers, have also tended in recent years to highlight the good of the pupil and their views generate further problems and distinctions. It would not be appropriate to go into all the intricacies here, but three broad positions are worth describing in brief. They have all been influential in the training of teachers and often underlie some of the teachers' opinions mentioned in the last two paragraphs.

The first view sees education as a process of 'growth' or 'development' towards a final end which is variously described as the 'cultivation of individuality', or 'self-realisation' or 'the fullest development of one's potentialities'. It is a biological model of education, likening it to something like the growth of a seed, given appropriate nurture, to a flower in full bloom. This kind of theory has been especially prominent in the training of nursery and primary teachers in the last fifty years and provides a rationale for some of the extreme forms of 'progressive' or 'child-centred' education, where teachers have fought shy of intervening too forcefully in children's learning for fear of upsetting the natural, i.e. biological, processes of their development.

The second view is found among critics of the first. They have poured cold water on the analogy between human learning and the biological development of plant or animal life, arguing that the goals of human life are not written into man's make-up in the way that the flower in full bloom is somehow prefigured in the seed. We cannot observe nature, that is, our own human nature, to find out in what our well-being consists. Neither is learning a process of natural development. It is essentially a *social*, not a natural, enterprise. To acquire any concept one must learn the rules which define its application to the world and its connections with other concepts. These rules, so it is argued, are *interpersonally* agreed, not the product of individual decision. So since concept-learning depends on social consensus and concept-learning plays so large a part in any person's education, education should be seen as a social undertaking. This is not, however, to say that it should necessarily have social *aims*, that, for instance, it should have less to do with the good of the pupil than with the good of society. It is only to say that the *procedures* of education cannot be left to nature: the teacher cannot stand back and let the child 'grow', but should see herself as intermediary between society and the child, deliberately intervening in his learning so as to initiate him into the publicly agreed rules which will shape his whole mental life. On the whole, most educational thinkers who have adopted this second, interventionist, position have tended, as far as *aims* go, to stick to pupil-orientated prescriptions. Personal autonomy, in one form or another, has been especially popular: they have argued that a central educational aim should be to produce children who think for themselves, who rely on reason rather than authority to substantiate their beliefs, and who, precisely because they think for themselves, work out their own plan of life according to their own lights, not swayed by the opinions of those around them (e.g. Dearden, 1968; White, 1973).

The third theoretical point of view relies in part on the second to come back to a position not far removed from the first. If, as the second theory claims, learning concepts is a matter of learning rules which are the product of social consensus, then what kind of conceptual equipment one acquires as one grows up depends on what the particular society in which one lives happens to agree about. This might well vary from one society to another, or from one sub-group to another: what counts as knowledge for a West European might be different from a West African's conception of it, and the same goes for middle-class as contrasted with working-class conceptions. Whatever conceptual schemes one teaches a child, therefore, cannot but involve the imposition of standards which are, in the last analysis, arbitrary. Education as we know it cannot become the intellectual liberation which the second theory idealises. It can only be at best a subtle indoctrination of a particular set of social values. The most influential way in which this thesis has impinged on the work of classroom teachers has been to make some of them wary of imposing so-called 'middle-class values' on working-class children. In some cases this has led to a rejection of areas of academic work on the grounds that they depend on a middle-class outlook and, sometimes, that concentration on such areas helps indirectly to preserve the social hegemony of the middle class and the capitalist system which supports it. One reaction to this fear of middle-class indoctrination has been to press for a specifically working-class form of education, culturally independent of middle-class standards. But since the charge of indoctrination would stick here too, since working-class children would then be indoctrinated into working-class beliefs and attitudes, many supporters of this third way of thinking would argue that the central educational priority is the liberation of the pupil from *any* arbitrary standards. This, if pressed, would lead them back to something like the first, non-interventionist, position described above. For if all standards are social and all standards are arbitrary, then the only way of avoiding arbitrariness is by jettisoning social influences and relying on nature. The individual, it seems, must be left free from social pressures of all kinds in order to work out his own values. In this way we come back full circle to the extreme 'progressive' or 'child-centred' view. And in fact as well as in theory we find close affinities among some Marxist or relativist teachers influenced by versions of the third theory and those influenced by the first. The common stereotype of the left-wing teacher as a woolly 'progressive' who lets children do what they want is 99 per cent misguided; but at the extremes it just touches reality.

The three educational theories just outlined have been born of the psychology, the philosophy and the sociology of education respectively. I shall be saying something about particular arguments later in this chapter. The main point in introducing them here has been to show that the dominant position of pupil-orientated aims found in parents' and teachers' conceptions of education is echoed in much contemporary educational theory. It is no exaggeration to say that until now the official wisdom among educators and educationists alike has been that education should centrally (if not wholly) promote the well-being of the pupil.

Two questions must now be faced. First, what *is* the 'well-being of the pupil'? We have seen how the term has been variously connected with such things as status, a 'good job', happiness, individuality, self-realisation and personal autonomy; all these connections need to be sifted through critically. Second, given that pupil-orientated aims are not generally considered to be the *sole* aim of education, how are they to be related to other aims? Neither of these questions is easy to answer and both will keep us occupied throughout this chapter and the next. In the rest of this chapter I will examine some answers to the first question.

First, then, what are we to understand by the claim that education should promote the pupil's well-being? What does this well-being consist in?

Basic goods

One point seems fairly uncontentious. There are certain basic goods which any person, and hence any pupil, will need simply in order to survive. He will need a minimum of food and drink, shelter, clothing, health care and so on. In a civilised country like our own we expect higher standards than this bare minimum. It is not mere survival that we care about, but survival after a certain fashion: we would like people to have *nourishing* food, *well-built* houses, *good* health and so on. There are also mental as well as physical basic goods: a certain degree of freedom from fear, for instance, of being left without adequate income to meet one's physical needs; freedom from drudgery or from tyranny. A certain degree of self-esteem, to take another example, has also been claimed as a basic good: without it a person is prevented, just as he is prevented by lack of food or shelter, from pursuing all sorts of valuable ends (Rawls, 1971, ch. 7).

There will be differences of opinion about *how much* of each kind of basic good should count as a reasonable minimum, and there may also be disputes about what things should fall under the heading of 'basic good'. But that food, clothing, health etc. are generally good for people I take as uncontentious. The difficulties arise when we move from basic goods to individual well-being in general. Basic goods are not normally thought of as goods-in-themselves, but as necessary considerations of well-being in the broader sense. I get my bad tooth filled not because having it filled is intrinsically valuable, but because unless it is filled I cannot get on with things that matter to me. Of course, the things that matter to me may themselves be means to further ends, like earning a living. But if I am rational this chain of means to ends cannot go on for ever: there must at some point be ends (or perhaps one dominant end) which are not means to some further end, but ends-in-themselves. Individual well-being cannot be confined, therefore, to the possession of basic goods, but must also embrace ends-in-themselves. This is not necessarily to say that *any* end-in-itself will do, since it is an open question, as yet, whether some ends-in-themselves are not more valuable than others. All we can say at this point is that individual well-being must embrace *good* ends-in-themselves. We may call these 'intrinsic goods', to differentiate them from the basic goods already mentioned.

How is all this to be related to the claim that education should promote the pupil's well-being? As I have hinted, the biggest difficulties will break out over what are to count as intrinsic goods: there is room for all sorts of controversy in this area and I shall come back to this in a moment. But given that basic goods are less contentious, in what way should an education which seeks to promote the pupil's well-being take account of them?

It should first of all make it clear to children what the basic goods are and why they are important. Sometimes this is obvious, sometimes less so. Every child will realise very early on that he needs food to survive, but it is not at all so clear just which foods are good for him and which are not and the child will often require explicit instruction in this. Health education more generally also comes under this heading. So does *some kind of* vocational education, given that a minimum income is a basic good and that income comes for most people, directly or indirectly, from a job. I stress 'some kind of' vocational education, because this term can cover many things and I don't want to be misunderstood. I am not implying here, for instance, that children should be trained for certain jobs or ranges of job, but only that they should come to see the importance to them of having enough to live on and be encouraged to think about ways of acquiring this. Now it may be that doing a job becomes a less prominent way of acquiring a minimum income in the future than it has in the past. If the futurologists who write about the leisure society which will grow out of the micro-chip revolution are to be believed, then only a minority may find themselves with a job and the rest be unemployed. Such a society *may* (although, of course, it need not) decide that people should be encouraged financially to stay out of work so as to reduce competition for the fewer jobs available. In this case, one may want to argue, pupils will not have to have their attention drawn to the need to ensure an income: the money will just fall into their lap even if they do nothing about it. But even here there will be different options open to pupils about how they acquire their income, first the big option between job or no-job and then, of course, options among jobs if a job is chosen. So some kind of vocational education in a very broad sense will be required even in the micro-chip utopia.

This is not the place to go into a comprehensive picture of the kind of education required to help the pupil understand the nature of basic goods and how to acquire them. In a more detailed planning of educational objectives much more would need to be said under this heading. Just one further point seems worth raising here. There is controversy, as already stated, about the minimum level of income, health etc. thought tolerable in a civilised society and also, perhaps, about what kind of thing counts as a basic good. (Food is a basic good, for instance, but need it include *animal* protein?) Since these topics are controversial, it would seem reasonable to make the pupils themselves aware of this fact. The question, for instance, 'At what level should one fix a minimum income?' is one upon which the pupil could at some stage usefully reflect. The alternatives would be either to ignore this basic good as irrelevant to his education, an option ruled out by the argument so far, or to impose on him some particular belief about what this minimum should be. Since to do so would be *ex hypothesi* arbitrary and unjustified, the original suggestion seems the most reasonable.

Intrinsic goods

I have said more than once that the concept of a basic good is less contentious than that of an intrinsic good. Even with basic goods, however, as we have just seen, controversy is unavoidable once one begins to speak of minima necessary *in a civilised society*, for what counts as a civilised society is open to dispute and therewith the basic minima. Is a bathroom (or TV or a washing machine or a car) a *sine qua non* of civilised existence? One's answer will be partly determined by one's views on the well-being of the individual in the wider sense.

(1)   *Progressivist views*
Among the several candidates for this, let us look first at the biological picture of human well-being found in the extreme progressivist or child-centred educational theory sketched above. In this picture our final ends are predetermined for us by nature: our well-being is a feature of the world, discoverable by letting nature guide our development. This assumption that human well-being is predetermined is one which the theory shares with most, if not all, theological accounts of education. In the latter, it is God who determines man's well-being; in the former, Nature. Progressivism, in such classic statements of it as Percy Nunn's theory of individuality, is a mirror-image of older, religiously based approaches to education which his new broom was meant to sweep away: science, in the shape of developmental psychology, rather than theology, was the new pathway to truth, and the good that it claimed to disclose had more to do with man's animal nature than with his eternal spirit; but in both it was a good not for him to create, but to discover.

These points are not of mere historical interest. The biological picture of education is still influential in many quarters; and so is the theological. Progressivist teachers and teachers in RC and C of E schools, as well as in the more theocentric of our public schools, often share this basic assumption that to know what our well-being consists in is to know something about the way in which our development is predetermined. But is this assumption justified? Again, if no good reasons are forthcoming, any educational recommendations built upon the assumption will be open to the charge of arbitrariness and teachers who propound them to the charge of imposing their own prejudices on their pupils. As I see it, this is in fact very often the case among the two sets of teachers just mentioned, the extreme progressive and the religious: they tend to work with a basic, unquestioned assumption about human well-being.

There are a number of apparently insurmountable obstacles in the way of any such justification. The theological account presupposes the existence of God; the progressivist, a purposive natural order. Neither of these things can be taken as read. But suppose they are conceded. On the theological side we are asked to accept the premise, which goes further, indeed, than what we have just allowed, that the good for man which God lays down is such-and-such. But how does one get from this premise to the conclusion that such-and-such *is* the good for man? There is, after all, a logical gap between 'God believes that X is good for man' and 'X is good for man'. One passes from a statement of psychological fact to a statement about values. The inference is, on the face of it, invalid. The progressivist faces a similar problem. His premise is something like 'Unfettered natural development leads the individual to X', where X is a purpose built into the natural order. But how does one get from this to 'X is good'? Here we start with a statement not of psychological but nevertheless of empirical fact and end up with an evaluative conclusion. Again, *prima facie*, an illicit inference. This is not to say, necessarily, that *all* passages from factual to evaluative propositions are illicit, although they may all be; only that these particular premises don't, as they stand, yield the desired conclusions.

Progressivism of this sort seems, then a non-starter. (I should make it quite plain that I am concerned only with progressivism *of this sort*. Many teachers who subscribe to the 'progressive' or 'child-centred' point of view limit this to *procedures* of education, not its aims. It is quite compatible to hold, as many teachers do hold, that children learn best when left maximally free to follow their own interests, while not believing that nature predetermines the ends they are to reach.)

Associated with progressivism, but also sometimes defended on grounds independent of it, are two further widespread pupil-centred beliefs: (i) that to cultivate individuality is to develop the *unique* qualities of individuals, i.e. those qualities which make them different from other people, and (ii) that education should seek to develop the individual's potentialities to their fullest extent.

(i) Parents and teachers often take this view as read. But it is not self-evidently true. Why should education foster individual differences rather than what men have in common? True, no one is going to argue that *only* individual differences matter: everyone will agree, for instance, that all pupils should grow up to be truthful and honest. But in so far as people *do* urge that individual differences are important, what grounds could they have for doing so? It is not easy to provide grounds. Part of the problem is that the claim makes most sense given a biological conception of development, i.e. given that different individuals have been endowed with different natural gifts, one with a musical ability, another with a constructive talent, and so on. There are problems, akin to those just discussed, about ascribing 'natural' abilities to people: one boy may be born with the ability to play the piano in the very thin sense that, unlike a child born deaf or without fingers, he is born with the ability to learn to play; but this is not at all to say that he is born with the ability to play where this implies that he knows how to do it. To say the latter is to imply that the standards and values associated with playing the piano can be implanted in us at birth, and this is again to imply the probably incoherent proposition that human values can be part of the furniture of the world. But, waiving this difficulty and agreeing for the sake of the argument that individuals do have different natural gifts, it still needs to be shown why these gifts should be cultivated. It needs to be shown, that is, why educators should work with nature rather than against her. If it is true that whatever attributes one is born with ought to be fostered, then it would follow that if we are born with a certain amount of innate aggressiveness, our parents and teachers ought to encourage us to be more aggressive. But it is irrational to think that merely because aggressiveness exists, it ought to be developed. One cannot argue just like that from an empirical fact to a conclusion about what ought to be the case. This applies to musical ability or constructiveness as much as to aggressiveness: that these things exist does not imply that they ought to be developed.

The doctrine of individual differences seems to be better grounded if one looks at individuals as members of the human species and argues, as Percy Nunn did, that evolutionary progress from species to species has depended on the emergence of unique, atypical individuals: the more one encourages individual differentiation the more one is acting as a handmaiden of nature in further evolutionary advance. Few today, perhaps, would want to justify the doctrine on these lines. As so often with educational theories, its popularity as an educational aim has outgrown the original rationale which brought it into prominence half a century and more ago. Not that this rationale was adequate, however. It presupposed the belief that natural evolution is a form of *progress*, i.e. that it leads towards desirable ends. This is to write a teleological element into nature which seems unwarranted. Why should we think that nature has purposes written into it? Perhaps its processes are blind and mechanical. Of course, if we make the old equation that Nature equals God and see evolution as part of a divine plan, we seem to get a little further along the road, as long as we posit the existence of God. But even if we *do* posit this, we still need to know that it is *a good thing* for us to follow the divine plan with all its supposed implications about fostering individual differences. It is not self-evidently so.

The philosophical argument could continue further in the theological direction. But let us stop it there and return to ask whether there is anything more to be said in favour of sharpening the differences between individuals. One argument, which is independent now of any biological implications, might be that a society containing a rich variety of individual activities and interests is more desirable than one without. This is an attractive claim. Most of us, I would guess, would prefer to live in the former sort of society. Whether this is in itself enough to show it to be more *desirable* depends on whether desirability is a function of preferences. But there may be other arguments, too, for the variegated society and I shall return to the issue in chapter 6 (see p. 126).

Suppose we accept for argument's sake that a variegated society is a good thing. Does it follow that educators should try to develop differences of talent and ability? Not necessarily. There is an alternative. In principle, at least, they could try to give all pupils the same broad education so as to acquaint them all with the whole range of activities and ways of life, from which they could choose their own. Given the unlikelihood of their all making identical choices, one would still end up with a variegated society. Are there any reasons why the approach via individual differences is to be preferred to this alternative? I cannot see any, but I know of one reason against. If education as a whole is such that a child with an aptitude for music, mathematics or whatever has that aptitude especially nurtured, then questions arise about the educator's *right* to shape the child's development in this specific way. The child, we may presume, is not in a good position to know what sort of life to choose before he has adequate understanding of the various alternatives open to him. But he is being steered in a certain direction before he reaches this point. On what grounds? In so far as this boils down to parental or other educators' preferences, then why should what parents or teachers want determine what children should do? If a parent wants his daughter to become a doctor, given certain aptitudes in that direction, why should what *he* wants be overriding? Why should it override what *she* might want to do when she grows up? It is simply arbitrary for a parent to steer a child in a certain specific direction because he thinks this is good for her. Indoctrination, once again, is not far away.

If it is better to determine one's own life than to have others decide it for one – and we shall be examining self-determination as an aim of education shortly – then we must leave it to pupils themselves to decide which of their abilities to develop as major constituents of a plan of life. This is not to deny parents the right to provide piano lessons for their children if they have an aptitude for music (let alone when they do not) or to encourage them to paint, play football, act or whatever. There are all sorts of reasons for their doing so which do not invoke the aim of sharpening individual differences: they might just want their children to enjoy themselves, for instance.

The doctrine of individual differences is often connected with the status-aims that we examined above. Parents sometimes want their children to develop special strengths which will put them at an advantage when competing in 'life's race'. The 'survival of the fittest' in the social struggle for a place in the sun is often seen as the survival of the most highly specialised: on this view the sooner parents can give their child help in this direction, the better. There is no need to add to what has already been said about the arbitrariness of steering children in specific directions which parents happen to favour.

One last point before turning to (ii). The strong point in the theory under discussion is, it seems to me, that we should emphasise in our education the pupil's uniqueness as an individual. I will be saying more in defence of this later on. But I do not see that this commits one to wanting to sharpen differences between individuals. A lot depends on what one takes as making one individual different from another. There are two ways of looking at this. Philosophers distinguish between 'numerical' and 'qualitative' identity. Two chairs may be *qualitatively* identical in that they share the same properties: they are both made of the same sort of wood, of the same design and colour etc. But they are not the same chair in that there are two of them. This is to say that although they are qualitatively identical they are not *numerically* identical. Now what makes one person different from another? Is it his possession of different qualities – physical characteristics, abilities, dispositions etc.? But suppose a pair of identical twins had exactly the same interests, abilities, tastes, thoughts and so on. They would be qualitatively identical, indeed, but they would not be numerically identical. What would make them different, then? What would their individual uniqueness reside in? The answer is, surely, that they are two distinct centres of consciousness: even though, *per impossibile*, they always had the same thought in their minds, twin A would have to be thinking the thought in his own mind and twin B likewise. So one can press for the importance of individual uniqueness without pressing for individual differences in ability etc. One can mean that we should urge each individual to see himself as a distinct centre of consciousness. As to why we should follow *this* as an educational aim, there might be several reasons. One has to do, again, with self-determination: one cannot autonomously determine one's plan of life without being aware of oneself as distinct in this way. More of this later.

(ii) The second, obviously related, aim is that pupils should develop their potentialities to their fullest extent. This is very often trotted out as a self-evidently valuable aim, but I wonder if those who do so trot it have always reflected on what it implies. It usually goes along with aim (i) and is open to the objections already made against that. But it goes further than (i) in its reference to 'the fullest extent'. If this is to be taken literally, it is not enough merely to develop a child's mathematical ability: this has to be nurtured right up to the limit; if he is capable of operating at PhD level or higher in mathematics, we must aim at his doing so. But why? Why should we want him to be *enormously* good at mathematics rather than just very competent? The claim, if taken seriously, seems simply arbitrary. And if we push it further and say, as many do, that we want the fullest development of *all* the child's potentialities, then what virtue is there in trying to ensure that he becomes a PhD (or more) not only in mathematics, but also, assuming he is able, in history, English, French, Russian, Czech, Polish, Rumanian, to say nothing of developing his powers of memory until he remembers the Bible off by heart – and backwards?

There are two ways of taking the thesis under consideration. One is to take it literally, as I have been doing so far. This assumes that there is a 'fullest extent' in the sense of an intellectual ceiling. The thesis is often conjoined with certain beliefs about IQ: ceilings vary among people along a normal curve and are fixed largely by heredity. The conjunction would then imply different terminal objectives in different children's education, since a few would have low ceilings, a few high ones and most somewhere in between.

A basic assumption of this position is that ceilings exist. It is difficult to see how this could be justified. To know that a person's ceiling is such and such is to know that he could not advance intellectually beyond that point. But how could we know this? One piece of evidence might be unsuccessful attempts made to try to get him beyond it. But *how many* unsuccessful attempts are necessary? If there have been X such attempts so far, the X-plus-first may yet succeed. The ceilings doctrine has not been put to such exhaustive and in principle limitless testing. It has simply been taken as read that it is true. But the claim that we each have ceilings (regardless of their origin, genetic or otherwise) is most probably unverifiable and certainly unfalsifiable. It belongs to the class of ideological beliefs – others are 'God exists' or 'all our actions are unconsciously motivated' or 'all historical events are predetermined' – all of which arc equally untestable and all of which, like the ceilings doctrine, find themselves the unquestioned first principle of ramifying networks of doctrine (White, 1974).

Even if ceilings do exist, there remains the question how one gets from this psychological fact to the normative conclusion that children ought to be educated so that they reach them. I do not know how the gaps in the argument might be filled in. Once again, the conclusion is often taken as read without one's having to bother with fiddly logical points like this.

The second way of taking the main thesis does not assume ceilings. The claim is now that pupils should be stretched as far as possible, where 'as far as possible' is to be interpreted within an assumed context, e.g. 'as far as possible within the next five years'.

The problems raised by this account I have already looked at: an intensive regime of this sort may be injurious to the pupil's well-being; and, in any case, no reason is given for pushing things as far as this rather than equipping pupils with a useful competence in various areas. Unless, of course, the thesis is conjoined with a theory about excellence: pupils should be stretched as far as possible at school in the hope or expectation that they will later become first-rate critical and creative thinkers. I have already looked at theories of excellence in chapter 2.

The general thesis in this section, which we have examined in its two interpretations, may also get entangled with two other educational views which are unexceptionable and which may therefore help to lend it plausibility. The first is that school children should be encouraged to do good work, to turn in well-thought-out pieces of writing, not to be satisfied with sloppy presentation, and so on. This is unexceptionable because being educated involves coming up to standards all along the line. But encouraging a child to do her best in this sense is not the same thing as pushing her to the limits of her capacities. The second view is that children should make progress in their learning. People sometimes argue vociferously about the need to stretch children to their full capacities when they hear of children, perhaps their own children, taught in mixed-ability classes, perhaps in a primary, perhaps in a secondary school, but making no headway because the class has to keep pace with the slowest. Again it seems to me reasonable that every child should be able to make some kind of progress. But stretching to the limits is another thing altogether. (For the bearing of the discussion in this section on the topic of university education, see below pp. 163–4.)

(2) *Happiness*

We cannot simply leave it to Nature to lead us towards the good. The progressives' reliance on Nature was a direct reaction to the older reliance on God. But it shared the same belief that man's ultimate well-being is wholly predetermined by something outside him.

Today many would hold the very different view that our well-being is of our own making. This is a Man-centred picture, not a God-centred or a Nature-centred one. It bids fair to dominate educational thought as it has philosophical.

It takes different forms. One of them identifies well-being with happiness. We saw earlier that the most popular aim in the primary teachers' survey was that children should be 'happy, cheerful and well-balanced'. These three terms may pick out rather different things and it is not known just how highly the teachers rated happiness as compared with, say, being well-balanced. But given that they did think it of great value, what did they mean by it?

There are two kinds of problem here. One is about the sense they attached to the word. The other is over whether they were thinking of the children *now*, as children, or as they would be when they were grown up. A few words, first, about this second problem. There are difficulties with both alternatives. If one's aim is only that children are happy now, then why is their later life to be left out of the picture? Suppose an emphasis on present happiness made them more likely to be unhappy later: why should the remoter future be sacrificed to the present? There is a similar arbitrariness in the other alternative: if happiness as an adult is all that matters, perhaps even at the cost of present unhappiness, then why is a later stage of life to be seen as more important than an earlier? The only way of avoiding the arbitrariness is to see each stage of life as equally worthy of consideration as every other. If happiness is to be the aim, or an aim, of education, it should be happiness in one's life taken as a whole.

But what is happiness? Sometimes the happy life has been equated with the life of pleasurable sensations. Huxley's *Brave New World* portrays a society where everyone is maximally happy in this sense, luxuriating endlessly in drug- or machine-induced satisfactions of the senses. A second interpretation is wider in scope. Here a happy life is one in which one achieves as complete a satisfaction of one's desires as possible. The things one desires may or may not include pleasurable sensations. The inhabitants of Brave New World would certainly be happy in this second sense, but so also would the weightlifter who goes through agony each time he lifts his bar above his head, or the doctor who successfully completes a lifetime of selfless and arduous service at a mission station.

I do not know of any educators who see their pupils' happiness as consisting in a life filled with pleasant sensations. Few philosophers, either, would equate well-being with happiness in this sense. What reason could there be for the equation?

The only remotely plausible one rests on a confusion. Some would argue that the ultimate reason why we do anything is for pleasure. The people of Brave New World do this directly. But it is true even of the doctor at the mission station: why would he devote himself to the sick unless he found pleasure in doing so? One implication of this line of thought is that all our behaviour must be egoistic: even where, as with the doctor, we take apparent examples of extreme altruism, these, too, are seen on analysis to be actions of a self-interested sort.

All this is muddled. It is possible, perhaps even likely, that the doctor experienced various pleasant feelings of satisfaction as a result of working among the sick. These may have included all sorts of bodily sensations. But the fact that he experienced these does not imply that he acted *in order to* experience them. This was not necessarily his reason for his behaviour even though it was its consequence. So it does not follow that all so-called altruistic reasons dissolve into egoistic ones.

Still, hasn't the doctor chosen the altruistic way of life for its own sake? And isn't this to say he is doing it *for pleasure*? And doesn't this help to show that the good must be connected with the pleasurable?

Not really. Or not in any way which identifies it with pleasant sensations. If I do something for pleasure, all this normally means is that

I do it *for its own sake* and not for the sake of any extrinsic goal like money or prestige. There is nothing in this use of the term about experiencing pleasant sensations.

There is more one could say about the theory that we can only act for the sake of our own pleasure, but it would be more profitable to turn to the *second* way of understanding the identification of well-being with happiness, since, unlike the hedonist way, this is currently very influential in philosophical and educational circles alike.[1]

How far, then, does one's well-being consist in as complete a satisfaction of one's desires as possible? As before, there is no good reason to restrict this to satisfaction now, or during childhood only, or during adulthood only: we are talking about one's life as a whole. A difficulty which some would see with this second view of happiness is that, like the first, it would seem to allow the highest human well-being to be located in the life of someone living in Brave New World. If all one's desires are maximally satisfied there, then how is any better state imaginable?

But what, after all, is wrong with Brave New World, if anything is? Many would say it is that its inhabitants have not been given the autonomy to determine their own lives for themselves: they have been *conditioned* to lead a life of constant pleasure and have not chosen this themselves.

This leads to a third educationally influential picture of personal well-being. Like the second version of the happiness theory, it identifies it with the satisfaction of one's desires; but it differs from it in also writing in autonomy.

(3) *Post-reflective desire-satisfaction*
It is a popular thesis of contemporary philosophy that the individual's good consists in the satisfaction of those desires which, *on reflection*, he prefers to be satisfied, given a full understanding of all possible options (Rawls, 1971, ch. 7). Educationally, this generates the aim of equipping the pupil to work out what he most prefers to do, e.g. by providing him with an understanding of different ends-in-themselves and seeing that he develops the disposition to make reflective and therefore autonomous choices (White, 1973).

An attractive feature of this view is that it seems to make the individual himself the final arbiter of his own good, not a blind follower of the authority of others, whether God or men. It underpins an education which avoids the imposition of value-judgments on the pupil:

he is not to be indoctrinated into others' pictures of the good, but freely chooses his own.

But there are problems.

(i) Suppose the reflective individual's most intense and most permanent desire turns out to be a desire for something very odd, like counting the blades of grass in a city park (Rawls's example). In structuring his life around the satisfaction of this want he is, on this theory, helping to achieve his highest well-being. The absurdity of this shows, one is tempted to say, that there must be something wrong with the theory.

What is it? Is it that it fails to do justice to the fact that ends-in-themselves are not all on a par, but that some are more worthwhile than others? The life of a dedicated scientist or composer, it might be said, would not give rise to the same charge of absurdity as the man's in the park. Does the pursuit of truth or artistic creation rate more highly than counting blades of grass?

If it does, then some reason has to be given. This might lead us back into the arguments about these kinds of intrinsic goods in chapter 2. In so far as these arguments are inadequate and no better ones are put forward to show that studying science, say, is more worthwhile in itself than counting grass, then we seem stuck with the view that any end can do.

This is one conclusion, then, about the theory: it seems to lead to absurd conclusions; but once one tries to put something in the place of the absurdity, one is in danger of embracing a perfectionist view that accords higher status to some ends than to others (and, educationally, leads back into the familiar problems of imposition and indoctrination).

(ii) A second, related, problem lies in the insistence on autonomy. The individual's choice of a way of life is to be autonomous, dependent on reflection and not simply adopted on others' say-so. But why is autonomy an essential ingredient in anyone's well-being? Before we can tackle this, we have to distinguish between two interpretations of the claim that the individual should autonomously choose his own way of life. (1) The first allows him autonomously to choose to be non-autonomous: after careful reflection, he decides to follow a life of servitude. (2) The second demands that the way of life he chooses embodies autonomy within it: it is not something which he can ever cast off.

Of these, (2) looks hard to justify as a universal prescription. Why should the individual be unfree to choose to become a soldier if this way of life most satisfies him? Why should he be compelled to remain autonomous even though this causes him great psychological stress? One answer could be that autonomy is valuable in itself for everyone. This would take us out of the non-perfectionist or 'democratic' theory of well-being on which we have been working, wherein no end is given an *a priori* superiority over any other, into a perfectionism which says some ends are of higher value than others. Once again, unless some further reason can be given for according autonomy this status, educators who aim at (2) may be charged with illicitly trying to impose on their pupils a particular way of life.

Do they avoid this charge if they retreat to (1)? They seem to, because they are not insisting that the pupil *remains* autonomous even if he has to choose his way of life autonomously in the first place. But what would they reply to a pupil who said, 'You say you've tried to avoid imposing particular ideals on me. But you've shaped me into an autonomous chooser. It could have been otherwise. I might have been brought up as a contented slave or Brave New World zombie. As a matter of fact I now prefer the autonomous life, but if my well-being consists in maximal satisfaction of my desires, how do I – or you – know that this would not have been more nearly achieved had I never been made autonomous? How can you justify having made me autonomous? Hasn't there been an arbitrary imposition on your part?'

(iii) The theory faces other difficulties, too. How is the autonomous chooser to decide which ends to follow? How does the pupil brought up under the *aegis* of this kind of aim choose his way of life? Innumerable doors have been opened for him; but what tells him which ones to go through? Is he to tot up anticipated units of satisfaction from different routes he might take and go for the one which gives him most? If not, what criteria does he use? Does he just 'plump' for a specific way of life with such-and-such constituent ingredients? There is nothing in the theory which gives us a lead. Many will say, teachers not least among them, that it is pretty vacuous unless it can be applied in the real world, but it is just how this is possible that is hard to grasp. Perhaps they are right.

(iv) A final difficulty lies not at the point of application, but at the other end, so to speak, in the justification of the theory as a whole. The pupil's well-being, it is said, consists in the satisfaction of those desires which, on reflection, he prefers to be satisfied. But why identify well-being with post-reflective desire-satisfaction? The identification is not self-evidently true. It is an empirical truth that such-and-such a way of life satisfies me on reflection, but is it an empirical truth that this way of life is *good* in itself? We seem to be moving from an empirical fact to a value-judgment. Desire-satisfaction and personal well-being seem to be things of logically different kinds.

All these objections may incline us to look at the pupil's good in a radically different way. All the theories examined so far have assumed that the good is *identifiable* with something else (with God's or Nature's purposes, happiness (in either of its senses), or post-reflective desire-satisfaction). But it is perhaps just this assumption that needs to be questioned.

How could it be questioned?

In two ways. One could maintain that the good cannot be identified with anything else; it is *sui generis*. The second way would be by jettisoning the concept of the good altogether as an unwelcome legacy from a theological age.

Does this second alternative make sense? What else would have to go if we tried to do without the concept of the good of the individual? We could talk neither about what is good in itself as far as he is concerned, nor about the basic goods needed *en route* to this. Neither could we talk about *moral* rules or virtues, assuming that as moral agents we should care about others' well-being as well as our own.

So much would be stripped away of ourselves as prudent and moral beings that it is hard to see what would be left. Would we become something more like a non-human animal, equipped by nature with certain goal-seeking potentialities which structure our behaviour, but not guiding our actions by any conception of our own or others' well-being? But we cannot conceive of ourselves still as human beings but so far lacking in self-awareness as to have no thought for anything but the satisfaction of immediate desires. We cannot help having some understanding of and concern about the future. Unless we commit suicide, we must structure out our future to some extent and according to some scheme of priorities. And this seems to make it inevitable that we employ the concept of personal well-being. Even if we commit suicide in this situation, it is hard to see how we can avoid thinking of this as *better* than its alternative.

(4)   *The good as* sui generis

If we cannot jettison the concept, can we adopt the first alternative, that whatever else we do not know about human well-being we *do* know, at least, that it is not to be identified with anything else one cares to mention, whether this be something very determinate like the pursuit of knowledge or less determinate, like the overall satisfaction of preferred desires? If we do, we now begin to have something of a purchase on a pupil-centred aim of education. As educators we may not be able to tell the pupil what his good is, but it does seem that we can warn him about what it is *not*. There is nothing which he can identify as his ultimate good, whether it be pleasure, material comfort, mystical experience, the pursuit of truth, or whatever. But this insight, negative though it is, by no means leaves him unable to plan ahead, to decide how he is to lead his life. For it can act as a practical guide, urging him not to commit himself wholeheartedly to any particular end if he does this under the mistaken belief that this constitutes his good. Its ability to guide his own behaviour applies also to his moral life. If others in his society are attaching themselves to particular ends in this same deluded way, he has just as much reason to try to prevent their committing themselves as he has to prevent himself.

It may seem that this argument leads into an impasse. To say that he does not attach himself to determinate ends under the impression that their achievement constitutes his good is to imply, it seems, that he must live constantly on a reflective plane, reminding himself of the peculiar nature of human existence, its absence of a *summum bonum* etc. etc. But is this not to make the reflective life his good? Is he not, in choosing to reflect, attaching himself to an end just as determinate as the life of a Don Juan or of a sybarite?

Can this difficulty be overcome? One could encourage the pupil to beware of latching on to reflectiveness in this way, teach him to distinguish between being reflective at times *in order to* avoid mistaking the good and erecting reflectiveness into a good in itself.

But what about the old charge that the educator here is just imposing his own value-judgments in an unwarranted way? Isn't he telling the pupil in effect that his well-being consists in *escape*, in not being caught, in not making mistakes about the good? Apart from the logical jam the educator now gets himself into − of seeming to imply that the pupil should escape from escape − there's also the point that this seems a very particular, not to say peculiar, view of human well-being: why should one's life be structured around not making mistakes of this kind? Something seems to have gone radically amiss.

All this assumes, in any case, that it *is* always a mistake to identify the good with anything else, that it is indeed indefinable or indeterminable. But suppose all philosophical arguments which concluded this are mistaken and there is, after all, some determinate content to our good. How wrong should we then be as educators in urging the pupil always to flee the determinate!

I think we must start again, if not from the beginning, at least from the position that the concept of the good seems indispensable and yet that it is hard to see what application one can give it. So far we have talked about the problems of *knowing* what the good is, *knowing* whether it exists in reality, *knowing* that it cannot be identified with particular prescriptions. This is to see it as something discoverable or undiscoverable. But perhaps this is to adopt an altogether too theoretical attitude towards it. There is another line of thought, very influential in education, which sees it as something to be *created*, not discovered.

(5) *Self-creation*

The individual – and in education, the pupil – now becomes much more like an *artist* than a truth-seeker, seeing his life as the expression of his deepest feelings and intuitions, rather as a Turner, say, conceives one of his paintings or a Wordsworth one of his poems. Percy Nunn puts this explicitly in his *Education*:

> Human lives, like works of art, must be judged by their
> 'expressiveness'. ... Our ultimate duty is not to let our natures grow
> untended and disorderly, but to use our creative energies to produce
> the most shapely individuality we can attain. For only in that way can
> we be, as we are bound to be, fellow-workers with the Divine in the
> universe (Nunn, 1920, p. 249).

I shall come back later to the religious justification in the last sentence. The artistic model of man as a self-creator is logically independent of it.

This idea has its origins in the eighteenth century, in Rousseau and in German Enlightment thinkers like Herder and Goethe and, later, Hegel and Marx. J. S. Mill's championing of individuality, which later found educational expression in Percy Nunn, owes an explicit debt to von Humboldt:

> The end of man, or that which is prescribed by the eternal or
> immutable dictates of reason, and not suggested by vague and
> transient desires, is the highest and most harmonious development of
> his powers to a complete and consistent whole (Mill, 1859, p. 115).

The artistic analogy fits well into our secular age. Man has no given good, so must create his own. He has, moreover, to create it *ex nihilo*. In a world without immanent values, he has to give shape to his life, give it, as von Humboldt says, a certain harmoniousness and completeness. This need not imply absence of conflict. Symphonies are built up out of contrasts and so are paintings and novels. But the artist can build these conflicts into the larger harmony of the work itself. So the good for man, on this model, is not a life of uniform and unvarying quality, but one which not only contains tensions between different inclinations within a larger whole but may even *thrive* on these tensions, just as the artist does, as a condition of its greater expressive power.

All this gives us a new way of looking at the pupil's good and at pupil-centred aims of education. If this is indeed how we should see human life, teachers and other educators now have an objective around which they can begin to structure curriculum content and other means of reaching educational goals. There are problems in making the simple inference that one good way of promoting self-expression in the way described is by letting the child engage in creative aesthetic pursuits – painting, drawing, writing etc. – but I shall bypass those, since I shall not be concerned until chapter 7 with the realisation of educational aims, but here only with elucidating the aims themselves.

How far, then, should educators try to get their pupils to see their lives as expression, as sharing the features just highlighted of works of art?

Can this theory, any more than any of the others, avoid the familiar charges of imposition and indoctrination? What of the articulate pupil who objects,

> I don't mind being left free to decide what kind of life I am to lead. But this idea goes further than that. It's telling me that I must aim at a harmonious life, one which transcends the conflicts built into it, etc. etc. But why should I go in that direction? I'm given no reason for it. Some people may want to shape their lives into sonatas or sonnets, and I'm happy for them to do so. But I'm not drawn that way myself. It's not only that anyone's life is so much at the mercy of contingencies that the idea of shaping it into a harmonious whole is hard to cash (there's nothing parallel in life to the potter's clay or the painter's pigments, which they keep under their control); more to the point, it's just not for me. I live much more from day to day – at the moment, that is: I'm not saying I always intend to, for that would, I agree, be to have some kind of life plan.[2] The main thing is that I don't

see why I should not be quite free to do what I want – to plan out my life as a whole, to live without a plan or even not to live, to commit suicide. Suicide is a good test of the artistic analogy. My teachers tell me I must create my own life. Suicide cannot be an option. They would see it as a cop-out, a kind of dereliction of duty. But I honestly don't see it that way. Why is suicide any *worse* than making one's life a work of art?

There may be a little confusion in this argument about the notion of a life-plan. There is no implication in the artistic analogy that one must structure out one's life with a clear picture from the word 'go' of what one is aiming at and how to go about achieving it. Works of art may sometimes be constructed in this way. But more typically, perhaps, especially with longer works, the artist begins with a very inchoate understanding of what he is after. This gains substance as he goes on, not achieving determinate embodiment as the work itself until after innumerable twists and turns, backtrackings, new beginnings. So it can be in life. Having a life-plan is not necessarily having a blueprint filled in detail from the start. The overall picture may well be built up gradually, shaped and reshaped by experience.

Is suicide ruled out by the artistic analogy? Perhaps suicide has its place in one's life-plan – the climax of the last movement of life's symphony, perhaps. Maybe one sees in the end that this is the only way one's life *could* finish and still make sense as a whole.

What the pupil is claiming, however, is the freedom not to *have* to see suicide in this way. He cannot see why he *must* be a self-creator. Why can't he drift if he wants to? Why can't he be free to make a mess of his life?

One answer would be that even if one believes that the best thing for him to be would be a self-creator, it doesn't follow that one must want to *compel* him to be one. It might be better, not from his point of view but from that of the wider community, to leave him free to do what he wants, even at the cost of his best interests: there are two conflicting considerations here – personal liberty and personal well-being – and there is no reason why the former should always be sacrificed to the latter.

This may seem to avoid the paternalism that the pupil was complaining of just now. But not really. If the ideal of self-creation has guided his education during youth even though he is left free to reject it at maturity, he *has* been compelled in that direction when young. In any case – and this goes to the heart of the problem – isn't there an inconsistency in saying that self-creation is a good thing, if one has built up the concept of self-creation on the premise that values do not exist? There is an obvious danger that self-creation is a purely personal ideal that may suit some but not others and yet that it may be presented as something necessarily valuable for all.

Perhaps we can test this by asking what justification there is for this ideal. Nunn gave a religious one – 'only in that way can we be, as we are bound to be, fellow-workers with the divine in the universe.' But if we do not accept a religious framework, what then? The onus is on the defender of the theory to give reasons why self-creation should be an ideal for everyone and not only for those who choose it.

(6)   *A positive view*

We seem to have run into the ground. After all these proposals and counter-proposals we are no nearer a satisfactory account of the good of the pupil. Is there any alternative left to us?

One thing we can do is to re-examine some of the fundamental issues in the theories we have already looked at, especially the theory that the good is identifiable with post-reflective desire-satisfaction. Four objections were made to that theory. Some of them were incomplete.

(i) The first objection, for instance, about the grass-counter, took it as read that he is an absurdity. The form of the argument was a reduction to the absurd: how could a man be in the highest state of well-being if he is counting blades of grass? But we have not pressed on to ask *why* this is an absurdity and it may now be appropriate to do this.

Why, then, is this an absurd case?

Rawls, whose example it is, suggests that it goes against a psychological generalisation about human beings, which he calls the 'Aristotelian principle' and which states that for the most part human beings prefer more complex activities to less complex ones (Rawls, 1971, ch. 7). Normally, therefore, a man would get bored with such a mindless task as counting blades of grass: he would prefer something more challenging. This is, it is true, only for the most part. Rawls admits that a man might choose to count blades of grass, but he would be an abnormal exception.

There are problems, adequately discussed in the literature, about Rawls's invocation of the 'Aristotelian principle'. It is highly doubtful whether men who know both chess and draughts will normally prefer chess. Many people would opt, if they could, to spend a fair proportion of their life on quite uncomplicated matters like strolling in the country or lying in the sunshine.

But the rights and wrongs of Rawls's particular arguments are less important than his appeal to an alleged feature of human nature. For human nature is something we have not paid much attention to in our more recent discussion of the pupil's well-being. It came up, of course, with extreme progressivism. Nature there was all-in-all: it predetermined our well-being completely. But after we dismissed that theory, we moved further and further away from looking at man as part of the order of nature. Of the various positions we looked at, the pleasure theory of happiness is at least tied to our nature in that it assumes a particular capacity, viz. to feel pleasant sensations, only found in beings of a certain kind, men included. If there are Martians, or angels, there is no guarantee that they are the sorts of creatures which can feel sensations. Questions about their well-being may still arise, but, if they do, this well-being will have to consist in something else. As we move on to the second version of the happiness theory, we drop talk of sensations, although we are still dealing with the satisfaction of desires. Leaving aside other animals, do only men have desires? Could there be other rational creatures, gods, angels, Martians or whatever, who can want things? Or is wanting dependent on having the kind of animal nature that men share with apes and cats and dogs? The answer is not clear. By the time we reach well-being as self-creation, we drop even the explicit reference to wanting. Man creates himself now *ex nihilo*. We have come close to something like the existentialist position which denies that human beings *have* a nature: they are all in their own making. But whether self-creation is only possible for a creature which has wants and whether these wants depend on an animal nature are, again, open questions.

To come back to the example of the man counting grass. Rawls suggests that this man is *unnatural* in preferring so simple a central end. Rawls may be wrong in his psychological theory, but it may still be true that we see the grass-counter as an absurdity because of what we implicitly know men are naturally like. One thing we do know about the grass-counter is that he could not have chosen grass-counting *in vacuo*. As a human being he has been born with all kinds of desires, including those which, like sexual desires, are at first latent but show themselves in due season. Ethological studies have revealed just how many of these innate propensities we share with other animals. We want to survive, we have sexual desires, we are curious, we are social animals enjoying the company of others, we dislike frustration and want to do things 'our way', we don't like to be stared at, we like attention, we like playing: the full list would be a long one. The grass-counter, if he is a normal human being, is equipped by nature with a whole range of desires, all demanding satisfaction. Of course, not all of them can always be satisfied without conflict between them. Human beings, like other animals, may both want to play and to survive, but survival generally wins out if they are in conflict, and the same for other desires. This example reminds us that nature helps us, too, to resolve such conflicts, weighting one satisfaction more than another in particular circumstances. The grass-counter comes, then, with such and such desires, conflicts between them and a natural interest in resolving these conflicts. This is not to say that all his desires, conflicts and resolutions are natural in the sense that they owe nothing to human institutions or human culture. That we acquire desires which other animals do not have is beyond question. Men can want to write novels, build space rockets and play chess. But all these wants are dependent upon and built up from more basic natural wants: a creature not interested in communicating with others, exploration or play would not have them. (For this whole line of thought, which has greatly influenced my thinking in this section, see Midgley, 1979.)

What are we to make of the grass-counter, given all this? We may assume him to have the normal array of natural human wants. No doubt, too, his culture has helped to shape these in particular directions. But what kind of priorities does he now have among them? Has he *no* place in his life for friendship, for art, for relaxation, for curiosity? Has he no other wants but this one? If he has none, then his case is indeed an absurdity, for human beings simply are not like this. We are creatures who possess as a permanent feature of our constitution a set of natural wants, shaped by culture into particular forms. We weight different desires differently and sometimes one sort may weigh very little. But there are limits to how far this can go. It is not within our powers to cut out every kind of desire but one from our lives. If this is indeed absurd, the only sense we can attach to Rawls's grass-counter is that he puts grass-counting high in his hierarchy of satisfactions: perhaps he still enjoys company, play, laughter, helping others and so on, but these mean much less to him than grass-counting. Perhaps, too, grass-counting is a rather unusual way of satisfying some natural wants: perhaps it gives him a sense of security, or perhaps it makes him noticed by other people. These things, then, would come to the top of his preference-hierarchy. But they still could not stand alone. As a human animal he will also want other things, although not so much. (Unless he wants them more: perhaps his grass-counting is an obsessive means of trying to repress his sexual fantasies.) If, then, the grass-counter has a whole array of desires, not just one, it is now not nearly so obvious that his well-being cannot consist in the satisfaction of what he most desires on reflection (i.e. definition (b)). For 'what he most desires' is to be understood not as one dominant desire, but as a graded pattern of different desires, and it might well be that as we heard more and more about what he wanted and why he wanted it, his preference for grass-counting in the context of other desires might begin to make much more sense. If the example is to be at all realistic, it will *have* to make more sense. Agreed, it is still difficult to see what could draw a man to such a way of life except for some religious reason or psychological necessity, but perhaps all this shows is that the example is, after all, too fanciful for us to take it seriously.

If all this is correct, then there may be more to be said than there seemed for the theory, that one's well-being consists in the satisfaction of one's preferred desires given that one has reflected on them.

(ii) The second objection to it was that its insistence on autonomy is unjustified. The main argument here was that once having been educated as an autonomous chooser the pupil might say that he preferred never to have become autonomous, so autonomy looks like an arbitrary imposition. We can now answer, in the light of the points just made about human nature, that steering a child towards autonomous choice is not at all arbitrary or unreasonable. He is a creature naturally equipped with wants, conflicts between them and higher-order propensities to resolve these conflicts. These wants are extended by human institutions and culture and, as they grow, so the possibilities for conflict grow too. He has to learn to cope with conflict, by establishing some kind of hierarchical order on his developing wants, to integrate them within a single scheme. To help children to become autonomous choosers is to encourage them to reflect on their wants in just this way, so that they are guided through life by a settled, integrated system of preferences. (Not that this will not be modified as they go through life in the light of experience: of course it will be.) If we fail to encourage their autonomy, what happens to them? There seem to be two possibilities. When their desires conflict, we may discourage them from trying to reach a solution, thus keeping them in a continuing state of conflict. This would be cruel and pointless. Or we could encourage them to resolve such conflicts, but not by autonomous reflection, but by blind reliance on authority in the shape, for instance, of parents, teachers, mass media or peer-group. Now no doubt it is natural to expect all children to rely to some extent on authority in this way, especially in their early years. But should one encourage them, as is now being proposed, to *keep on* doing this into maturity rather than moving gradually towards autonomy? Would there be any good reason for this? One would have to be able to show that those on whom they relied always knew best how to resolve other people's desire-conflicts. But although some people know more than others about (some of) the consequences of taking this line of action rather than that and some people have reflected more than others on the ethics and psychology of personal choices, there is no body of expertise which can allow one person to say of another: 'Given that he wants both to do A and B, and that the consequences of doing A are such and such and the consequences of doing B are such and such, then he ought, on balance, to do B, not A.' There are no ethical experts when it comes to making judgments of this sort. We can turn to others for *advice* (which presupposes that we are ultimately autonomous), but not for authoritative pronouncement. If so, to come back to the main issue, educators have no good reason to bring up their pupils believing that they should rely on authority when faced with conflicting desires.

So encouraging autonomous choice is not at all an arbitrary imposition on a pupil. It is easy enough in the abstract to excogitate a hypothetical pupil who is supposed to object that he might, for all he knows, have been better off if he had been a slave or a Brave New World zombie; but once one fleshes him out with a real human nature it is difficult to make sense of him: unless, that is, his plea is an expression of unresolved conflict. He may simply be envious of those whose minds lack the tensions that he experiences. But what he needs in this case is *more* practice, not less, in reflecting on his wants and getting them into some kind of order.

How far does all this give educators a reason not only to bring their pupils up so that they reach an autonomous state but also to encourage them to *remain* autonomous once they have reached it? It does not give, as I see it, a strong enough reason for their continuing always to be autonomous come what may. For there may be cases where remaining autonomous has itself to be weighed in the balance against a non-autonomous alternative – say becoming a slave or committing suicide. Perhaps the autonomous way of life will become too burdensome in some cases and the individual's last autonomous act will be to rid himself of that autonomy. This possibility must always be left open for him. But this does not then mean that the only thing the educator can do is to say to the pupil once he is autonomous, 'It's all one to me what you do with your life: I've no strong feelings either way whether you remain autonomous or whether you don't.' He has good reasons to care that the person he has brought up to be autonomous stays that way, unless he finds the burdens of autonomy too great, reasons to do, as before, with the conflict-ridden nature of human life, the need for some kind of resolution and the misguidedness of trying to find ethical experts on whom to rely.

(iii) We can now also face the other objection to the theory, that it gives no guidance to the pupil about *how* he should choose his way of life: by what criteria does he select from the ramifying options before him? Does he just 'plump'? From what we have just seen, choice is not at all a matter of sticking a pin in a list of possible satisfactions. One chooses against a background of wants which one already has, the most basic of which are part of one's natural constitution and inalienable. Choosing is weighing relative importances, preserving a balance between different satisfactions so that natural needs – for sociability, security, honour etc. – are not thwarted. Is the secure life of a civil servant going to prove satisfying to me in the long term? Or will it get too much in the way of my natural predilection for novel experiences or my ambition to make a mark on the world? I can only think this through in the full knowledge of what kind of creature I am and what sacrifices I would be making in other parts of my nature if I adopted a particular course of action. But it *is* a matter of thought, not of mindless plumping. And to a very great extent the thought I put in is influenced by the thinking of others, as expressed in the commonsense wisdom of my community and the insights of writers and philosophers. It is not I alone who have conflicts between security and freedom, between intellectual interests and sociability, between fame and altruism or between a serious concern with things that matter and a desire to poke fun at it all. These tensions are part of human nature and have always existed, if not always in the same sophisticated form. Men have reflected on these conflicts for millenia: the fruits of their thinking, in literary or other form, can guide us in our present choices.

So the third objection, that the chooser is left without guidance, also goes once the theory is conjoined to an account of a specifically *human* nature and is not left as something so general in its application that it could fit gods, angels or Martians who lack our peculiar make-up.

(iv) We are left with the fourth and last objection, to do with the justification of the theory as a whole. Why is personal well-being to be identified with desire-satisfaction (given reflection)? No reason has been offered for this, and there seems to be at least one powerful reason against it. The two terms seem to be of logically different kinds: whether such and such a life is satisfying is an empirical matter, to be decided by observing how things are, but whether such a life is good in itself introduces a question of value.

It is because the concept of the good seems irreducible to empirical concepts like desire-satisfaction that philosophers have turned to anti-naturalistic accounts of human well-being, to do with self-creation *ex nihilo*, for example. But *is* it irreducible? A difficulty here is that our present concept of human well-being is a concept with a history. For most of its existence it has been incorporated within theological pictures of man and his place in the universe, or more recently within anthropocentric doctrines which put Man rather than God at the centre of things but still, as with the older theology, stress the uniqueness of man in the natural order, his unlikeness to other animals. For most of its history, then, human well-being has been seen in religious terms, divorced from and opposed to the satisfactions of our animal existence; and even when the religious view was replaced by the anthropocentric, the old reluctance to identify well-being with animal satisfactions persisted. So it is not really surprising that we should see a conceptual gulf between desire-satisfaction and the good. On the traditional conception of the good there is no doubt that such a gulf exists. But the important question is: need we work with this traditional conception? Cannot we reject it as a confusing hangover from our theological past?

Once one begins from the other end, seeing human beings as a kind of animal, equipped like other animals with an array of possibly conflicting desires, and whose specifically human form of life with its complex institutions of language, morality, government, science and the rest has been built up around and developed from these natural desires – once one looks at man fairly and squarely as a kind of animal rather than a god manqué, it becomes increasingly hard to see what account of a man's well-being one *could* give except in terms of the satisfaction of his desires, not only those which he possesses by nature but also those which his culture introduces him to, taking his life as a whole and given that he has reflected on the conflicts inevitably arising between these desires in order to establish some way of ordering them within an integrated life plan. Perhaps we cannot give up the concept of the good, even though it has come down to us *via* doctrines we find no longer acceptable: we have to regulate our lives according to *some* concept of our own well-being. But there is no reason now, given a reassessment of our relations to the rest of the natural world, why we should not see it in terms of satisfying the demands of our nature.

If this will do then there is no need to reject the post-reflective desire-satisfaction theory and look for quite other accounts of human well-being, e.g. as something essentially undiscoverable or as self-creation *ex nihilo*. There are features worth retaining, however, from both these accounts, as long as these are *combined* with the desire-satisfaction theory and not seen as alternatives to it. The first of them told us that the good is a mysterious thing, undiscoverable but none the less existent: in seeking it, we have to avoid the temptation of thinking that we have discovered it, by identifying it with particular prescriptions – the life of artistic endeavour, of reflection, social service, a mixture of all these three, or whatever. The naturalistic perspective takes away a lot of the mystery. But not all of it. Human beings are *different* from other animals as well as similar to them. They are different both in having, via cultural influences, a vastly more complex array of desires which could be constituents of their way of life, and, of course, in being obliged, given their peculiar form of intelligence and their self-awareness, to think through priorities and impose some kind of integrating structure on their desires. How should they do this? What should guide them in establishing their priorities, in making their trade-offs and balances? I have already acknowledged the help which both nature and human culture can give here, but this does not settle everything. The individual himself must make the ultimate decisions. And in describing how he is to do this it is hard to avoid the metaphor of *depth*. He has to dig beneath his surface inclinations, steel himself against unthinking acceptance of ideals of life which he has picked up from others, penetrate to more fundamental layers of his being, to his 'deepest needs'. Complete self-knowledge will reveal to him his most basic orientations.

But suppose there is nothing at the bottom of the barrel. Can we *discover* our deepest selves? Or is self-*creation*, after all, a more appropriate description? It is nonsense to say that we create ourselves *ex nihilo*. We have a human nature. But ours are still the ultimate choices and if at some point we can dig no further into ourselves, what else *can* we do but *construct* our way of life out of the materials which nature has given us, following the guidance which past generations have bequeathed us? The artistic analogy *is* apposite, to a point. A work of art is an integrated whole, a harmonising of diverse and conflicting parts. So is a human life. Neither works of art nor human lives construct themselves, or are constructed by nature. They both need an originator.

Ultimately, perhaps, we cannot adjudicate between man as self-creator and man as self-discoverer. We may do worse than to revert to the old notion of human life as a process of self-realisation, relying on the Janus-faced character of this concept, with its suggestions both of coming to know oneself and of working out a self-determined plan.

How far, then, can we accept the post-reflective desire-satisfaction theory as the definitive account of the good for man? It has stood up to a number of objections. But are there others?[3]

(1) The theory sees individual well-being as the satisfaction of those desires which, on reflection, one most wants to be satisfied. But in the course of one's life, one's preferred desires may change, even radically. So what one takes to be one's well-being at any one time may come not to seem so at a later time when one's preferences have altered. Which of the two patterns of satisfaction, A and B, constitutes one's good? If one of them does and the other does not, by what criteria are we to determine this? The post-reflective desire-satisfaction theory will not help, since both cases already meet its conditions.

One answer to this is that one's good is constituted by desire-satisfaction over one's life as a whole, not at such and such discrete points in it. If one succeeds more or less in satisfying one's desires in the earlier pattern, A, and also succeeds more or less in satisfying the radically different pattern in B (and so on for C, D and any later changes), then one has by and large lived a life of well-being. There is, therefore, no need to bring in criteria lying outside the theory we have been working with.

Even so, there remains the doubt that what one *thinks* is one's good, even taken over one's life as a whole, may not be so, in fact. What is it to say this? That if one had lived for as long again one might have radically changed one's preferences? This would be something like the transition from A to B. In discussing that, we took it that the satisfactions in A were not to be discounted as part of one's total well-being, even though they were rejected in B. One's life-time's satisfactions, taken as a whole, are similarly not to be discounted. It is true that one cannot, finally, say what one's well-being *is* as distinct from what one *thinks* it is. But this should not be a cause for concern. It is only a reflection of the truth we have already noted in the idea of self-creation. Ultimately, given all we have said about the basis of our well-being in our natural wants, ours are still the ultimate choices. We can only do what we can. When we have thought through our life-plan as comprehensively as possible, there is nothing more we can do to discover our well-being. The idea that we are only in the world of appearances and that reality still lies outside may still haunt us. But this is a ghost of ancient, e.g. theological, theories of the good which we are no longer constrained to accept.

(2) A second objection brings us back to our earlier discussions about whether the post-reflective desire-satisfaction theory did not put too much emphasis, for some tastes, on reflectiveness. It seems to enjoin us to spend a lot of time working out a life-plan. Ideally, we have to know about all the ends available to us as options, to reflect on the means of achieving them and obstacles in their way, to work out a settled scheme of priorities, given what we know about the consequences and implications of following this course rather than that, etc, etc. This enterprise itself, one may be tempted to say, may well last as long as a lifetime. Just to take the first item, knowledge of all available ends: there are simply just so many of these, especially if we look at sub-categories as well as major categories (among card games alone, we will have to know about patience, poker, whist, bridge and then what about the sub-varieties of each of these?).[4] If we push things as far as this, we reach *one kind of* ideal of life, one which devotes a lot of time, perhaps an indefinitely expanding amount of time, to working out one's plan. But not everyone need follow such an ideal; and, indeed, it may be ridiculous that *anyone* should. The theory puts too much emphasis on *reflective* choice, not doing justice to the fact that very often our choices may be more impulsive. There is no reason why the more reflective life should be closer to the good than the more impulsive life. The theory overlooks the extent to which we are *drawn into* ways of behaving, activities, modes of life *before* we have reflected fully on our life-plan. To insist that young people do not commit themselves to any particular activities as part of their total way of life until *after* they have worked out their life-plan is to fly in the face of human nature. Should a 12-year-old girl who has come to love music, say, keep her commitment to it lukewarm until, several years later, she is in a better position to decide whether or not she still wants to incorporate music into her life-plan? Why should she not throw herself into it wholeheartedly? Isn't the theory a recipe for producing young persons who have no enthusiasms for anything ... except, of course, for working out life-plans?

Part of this objection can fairly easily be accommodated within the theory. Having a life-plan does not rule out spontaneity or impulsiveness. One might build into one's plan that it include an area of spontaneity, just as some people, but not all, plan their annual holidays to allow themselves the freedom to indulge whatever whims or fancies they then happen to have. But this answer does not take us very far. For what is basically at issue is, on the one hand, the reflective ideal and, on the other, an unwillingness to rule out, as constituents of one's well-being, commitments which are less the product of reflection than of being drawn into, fascinated by, perhaps even being taken over by, activities or projects of different sorts.

What I think this shows is that one should not press the post-reflective desire-satisfaction theory too far in the reflective direction. Its name refers, after all, to desire-satisfaction as well as to reflection, and we should not lose sight of the important point made earlier, that the desires which we are to satisfy are already given to us to a large extent as embedded in our human nature. If, for instance, the satisfaction of curiosity is a nature-given constituent of our well-being, then if a child gets – unreflectively – fascinated by, say, physical science, there is surely a *prima facie* reason for saying that, in extending her natural inclinations in this direction, she is, to put it at its least, not going against what constitutes her well-being. Looked at from this end of the theory, that is from human nature and not from the demands of reason, *of course* we should not try to prevent children developing enthusiasms. At the same time, there is no need to push the reflective ideal to the limit of ridiculousness whereat ensuring that pupils know all the sub-categories of sub-categories of ends takes precedence over ensuring that they have genuine commitments. I have talked above about our need to strike a balance between conflicting desires. This is only another instance of the same point. On the one hand, we want enthusiastic engagement in things; and we want these throughout our lives, childhood included, not only after we have reached the age to decide on a settled life-plan. On the other, we want children not to be imprisoned within a narrow range of life-options, but to reflect on their life as a whole, having become aware of all possible alternatives. If we push either too far, we get narrowness of vision in one case and a crazy search for comprehensiveness in the other. Somewhere between them we must strike a balance. There is good reason for weighting things more heavily on the side of commitment, of enthusiasm. For reflectiveness is here not an end in itself, but subserves desire-satisfaction. *Primarily* we should do the things we most want to: that is what life-planning is all about.

Pupil-centred education: the two-fold task

If educators are to aim at promoting the good of their pupils, their work is twofold, partly a matter of enlarging understanding and partly to do with shaping dispositions to behave in certain ways.

The pupil has to understand in general terms what his well-being consists in. He has to see himself as an animal with such and such an array of natural desires and to appreciate the way in which these desires may take different forms owing to cultural influences and new desires of all kinds be built up out of them. In introducing him to this enormous range of human desires, his education is *expansionary*. In another way, it is *restrictive*. He is not to choose his way of life from this smorgasbord *ad lib*: he must know, too, about the *permanence* of his natural desires – his wanting to be loved, to be secure etc. – and about the need to hold all his desires together in an integrated unity, structured around these permanent dispositions and incorporating the autonomous balances he strikes between conflicting demands of all kinds.

All this is to do with his well-being in its final sense, as an end-in-itself. Earlier on, we also discussed basic goods, i.e. things which are necessary conditions for pursuing any ends-in-themselves – a minimum of money, health, shelter, food, clothing and so on. The pupil must have some understanding of basic goods. More broadly, he needs to know about what means he can adopt to attain his ends. There would be no point in acquainting the pupil with what his final well-being is if one gave him no understanding of what he has to have in order to attain it. What is necessary depends to some extent on what precisely is included in the final end. If collecting antiques is a constituent in this one needs to have a lot of money, but other ways of life might demand less. And so on. For all the variation, there will be certain constants: for one way of life one may need to be physically fitter than another, but for any way of life one will need a certain minimum of physical health. Among goods as means should also be put such self-regarding virtues as courage, temperance and wisdom. These are not material necessary conditions like shelter or money, but have to do with the regulation of desires, with their ordering and integration. Without them, as without food or shelter, the pupil could not attain his final ends. So he has to understand *their* place in his life also.

He will also need to know what kinds of *obstacles* he faces in seeking his final good. These can be of various sorts. There are psychological impediments. He may lack the ability or temperament needed for particular options. Or he may be beset by neurotic anxiety or other form of mental ill-health, which may get in the way not only of particular ways of life but also of the reflection he must engage in in deciding his life-plan. There are socio-economic obstacles also. His chances of taking up the professional career he sets his heart on may be limited in different ways: there may be great competition for such jobs and their number limited; and some groups of pupils, of which he is not a member, may have special advantages in this competition, e.g. those from public schools. The way in which work institutions are organised – whether on authoritarian or democratic lines – may be seen as helping or hindering him in his choice of a way of life. These are only examples. There are all sorts of other socio-economic obstacles, too. The running-down of vital world resources may hinder the ways of life which young people today may decide upon, and it is important that they have some understanding of it. Many other examples could be given.

One reason why I stress this knowledge of means and impediments is that once these are weighed in the balance they will help to shape the pattern of final ends which the pupil adopts. What he might have wanted to do in an ideal world has to be scaled down to fit realities and probabilities. His reflective integration of a life plan is even more complicated – but by no means more difficult, since the choices are no longer wide open – than it seemed when we were discussing only ends-in-themselves. A new conflict enters the picture – the conflict between the ideal and the realistic. New balances will have to be struck between the rival demands. Once again, he is not left on his own. He can find guidance in novels, in biographies and elsewhere. But how he finally strikes the balance is his decision alone.

It should be obvious from all this that his understanding of means and obstacles should be both general and particular. He needs to know the sorts of things in general which help or hinder *anyone* and he needs to know which *particular* obstacles he faces in his specific situation in the world and which *particular* means he can expect to be available. Neither knowledge would be much good to him without the other.

So much for the enlargement of understanding. The other aim is to do with shaping dispositions. Understanding alone is not enough. In principle one could acquire all the different kinds of understanding just sketched – of the variety of possible ends and the natural restrictions on these, of basic goods and obstacles, general and specific, of the conflicts which arise between desires and the need for integration – but still do little or nothing about it all: it could remain at the level of theoretical knowledge. To give the pupil no more than this is to do him a disservice, for what he also needs is to acquire the various dispositions, or self-regarding virtues, which enable him to fit all this together into a unified whole. He needs courage to prevent his being dominated by fearful desires when his long-term good opposes this, temperance to keep his bodily desires within bounds; patience; strength of will; a good temper. He also needs to acquire the reflective disposition necessary to integrate the whole gamut of his desires, to strike the right balances when they conflict. Counterbalancing this should be the disposition to act on these desires, to throw himself enthusiastically into his projects and not to leave himself, Hamlet-like, eternally reflecting but never committed to anything.

How one builds up these dispositions is another matter. With some qualification in the case of the last disposition described (since this is so much a part of our nature-given selves), this is bound to be a slow and gradual process. It must go hand in hand with the acquisition of the various sorts of understanding: in many ways the twin aims will be from a practical point of view inseparable. Of the two, dispositions take priority, given that an education with the pupil-centred aims we have been describing is a matter of bringing children up to be a certain sort of person. The possession of knowledge or understanding is not an educational end in itself, but without it the necessary dispositions could not be formed.

Chapter 4

The good of society (1): economic, moral and pupil-centred aims

Should education be directed towards the good of the pupil alone? Few think so. There is the good of society to be considered, too, whether one has in mind economic goals or the pupil's moral obligations. While not neglecting these, parents, teachers and educationalists have tended of late to put pupil-centred objectives in the centre of things. Is this justifiable? What pattern of priorities should there be among competing aims?

Economic aims and pupil-centred aims

The education system is sometimes treated, especially by politicians, partly as a means of maintaining or improving the economic life of the country, by helping to provide the kinds of workers required in different sectors and equipped with the right kinds of qualifications, abilities and attitudes.

This aim is often at odds with pupil-centred aims, not least with the kind of positive aim sketched towards the end of the last chapter (see also Edgley, 1980). This aim expands the pupil's horizons, seeks to make him master of his destiny : but an economy-centred education may well try to restrict his expectations, trim them down so that he fits as neatly as possible into an occupational role. The conflict can become especially acute if one remembers just how many millions of jobs in our kind of 'advanced' industrial society are pretty unattractive, not at all the sort of thing which anyone would be likely to include as a permanent part of his life-plan if he had a full choice of alternatives. These include not only dirty, arduous or dangerous jobs like mining, road-repairing or humping bags of fertiliser, but also the tediously repetitive and mechanical jobs produced by extreme division of labour through technological advances, like work on an assembly track or at a supermarket check-out or, increasingly, in offices.

The economic aim can conflict with the positive pupil-centred aim in different ways. First in the kind of knowledge and understanding it requires. As we saw, the pupil-centred aim demands a very broad understanding of varied ends, means to ends and so on. The economic aim demands only what is necessary to a particular kind of job or range of jobs. For some jobs it demands specialists who know a good deal about such things as mechanical engineering, marine biology, industrial psychology etc., but it provides no reason why they should know anything else. For those jobs – the majority – which require little or no specialised knowledge which cannot be picked up in a few days or weeks at work, it demands very little knowledge. A basic literacy and numeracy are all that are necessary: the more an individual attains beyond this point the more his widened horizons may make him *dissatisfied* with the tedious job he will have to do.

The two aims also conflict over the dispositions they encourage. The pupil-centred aim promotes reflectiveness, the economic, at least in the familiar form now under consideration, a ready obedience to authority. Considered only as units of labour in industrial and other enterprises as we currently know them, workers do not need to reflect on the rights and wrongs of what they are asked to do. Reflection, too, may breed dissatisfaction and the smooth running of the company may suffer. This is why economically oriented controllers of educational systems often put such a price on the pupils' bowing to the authority of their teachers and favour authoritarian structures in school organisation. It also explains why they like the rote-learning of such subjects as arithmetic and foreign languages. Those who train army recruits know the value of drill in breaking men in, in getting them to do things to order and without question. Rote-learning in school can be used for the same purpose.

But the most important way in which the two aims differ is this. The pupil-centred aim requires that the pupil himself internalises the aim, sees it and accepts it for what it is. He cannot become an autonomous planner of his own life without coming, perhaps gradually, to know that this is what his educators are aiming at for him, and without accepting it as what he wants. But this is not at all necessary to the economic aim. That the pupil knows and accepts the aim of maintaining or improving the economy is not a part of the aim itself: it is enough that he is equipped for and has the approved attitudes towards a job in a particular sector of that economy. For reasons just stated, it may well indeed be *counterproductive* to let him in on the aims of his education. If he knows, he may resist. He may not want to be steered into a meaningless job or welcome the limiting of horizons which specialisation can bring. His ignorance can give his educators more scope to win his compliance by stealth.

What can one do in the face of this conflict of aims?

One can be an ostrich and try to ignore it. One way is by fixing up one's concept of education in such a way that the conflict doesn't arise. Education is defined as something with only intrinsic aims, the pursuit of knowledge for its own sake, for instance. Economic aims must therefore fall outside it. The educator as educator has nothing to do with them. Other concepts come into play here: *training* in specific skills for specific ends, and *socialisation* into the mores expected in the work-place. But training and socialisation fall outside the province of education.

This is tidy, but it solves no problems. Apart from raising all the difficulties with restricting education to intrinsic aims which we discussed in chapter 2, teachers and other educators are still left with a conflict between educational aims as redefined and economic aims. This will not now be a conflict of *educational* aims, but the conflict will still be there for all that.

Another response to the conflict is *compromise*, the 'render unto Caesar' approach. A good example of this at work is found in the survey of primary teachers' aims mentioned in chapter 3 (Ashton *et al.*, 1975). It discovered that their views on aims tend to lie on a continuum. At one extreme teachers believe that 'education is the means used by society ... to ensure that new generations will maintain it both practically and ideologically' (p. 11). Such teachers 'rate as most important aims dealing with the basic skills and with conventionally acceptable social behaviour' (p. 12). At the other extreme 'is the view that education is a personal service to the individual' (p. 11). Here the aims thought most important are 'concerned with developing independence, both emotional and intellectual, and with a much broader educational front, including art, music, movement, drama, and so on' (p. 12). Few teachers, we are told, are exclusively attached to one of these extreme positions: 'the great majority hold both to some extent' (p. 11), but with differing emphases.

The tension described is immediately recognisable. So, too, is the compromise which many teachers seem to settle for, i.e. to pay a certain amount of attention to basic skills and in the rest of the time to foster the child's personal development by allowing him plenty of choice among *activities*, especially creative activities; a régime, for instance, of reading and sums in the morning, 'choosing time' in the afternoon.

There are all sorts of problems about the *particular* kind of compromise here involved, especially about the aesthetically orientated conception of the pupil's well-being. But a general defect which this shares with other similar compromises is that no attempt is made to *re-late* the two kinds of aims and therewith the curricular activities they give rise to. They each are given their due, but at what cost? The fact that they conflict fundamentally is not squarely faced.

Primary schoolchildren are far enough removed from having to face going to work that the conflict can be swept under the carpet for the time being. Secondary schools find things more difficult. For some pupils, the quicker and more knowledgeable, a new kind of resolution is at hand – specialisation. The economy needs specialists (including, it is said, arts specialists for posts in the Civil Service and elsewhere). If the pupil specialises, taking public examinations in his specialism and pushing upwards through the system as far as he can go, he can hope to get a 'good job' and the income and status that go with it. If his personal well-being is seen largely in 'good job' terms, the economic and pupil-centred aims can lock nicely together. But we have seen grounds for looking at one's own well-being in a far more liberal way than this. The more stress one puts on breadth of vision as a constituent, the more this form of compromise becomes unstuck. There is only the appearance of a resolution: the real tensions lie buried underneath.

But all this applies, in any case, only to the academically successful. What about the rest? For them there is not even an emasculated well-being which can incorporate the economic aim within itself. Their desire for a life of their own faces starkly the knowledge that, unless they are lucky and make a go of minicabbing or odd-jobbing, a life of industrial semi-serfdom is before them. It is not at all surprising that older pupils become troublesome when they realise this. Who *could* accept this situation with equanimity?

Supporters of the socio-economic status quo have, not surprisingly, always been exercised by the problem of coping with those troublesome youngsters who refuse meekly to bow to the inevitable. Is there any way of bringing their personal ambitions into line with industrial demands? One school of thought favours something like a continuation of primary-school practice, combining attention to obedience-training and rote-learning with, on the personal side, various aesthetically inclined activities, like movement, drama, arts and crafts. This is sometimes linked with a theory of intelligence which claims that the great majority of pupils lack the ability for tougher intellectual work and require an 'education of the emotions' based on aesthetic activities. But this line gets nowhere. It still does not show how the opposing aims can be resolved. A vision of a factory community where operatives work away happily in a world of piped music and pleasant day-dreams is no answer.

The more 'realistic' solution, especially in an egalitarian age, is to try to give as many pupils as possible the chance to compete in the examination stakes which have always been the passport to a 'good job'. Specialisation via the examination system has been one way of bringing personal and economic goals into line, but it has until recently only been for the 'bright'. But if *nearly all* children work for examinations, choosing which subjects to specialise in, then the same resolution should be possible on a far wider front. Provided, of course, that the economy still gets the kind of workers it wants in the less favoured jobs. ...

And this, of course, is the rub. It might well be possible to cut down antipathy among the 14–16-year-olds by putting more and more of them on to the examination escalator. But this might raise their expectations too high for the kind of job they can reasonably expect. There are ways of plugging this hole, too. One can try to steer them towards examinations that don't get them anywhere, like the CSE (unless they are lucky enough to get a grade 1, since only this is equivalent to an O-level pass). This is a cynical confidence trick since it makes pupils believe that they are working away for their own advantage just like others doing O or A level, whereas they will be obliged in the end to take a humdrum job because when they enter the job market they will find themselves inadequately qualified.

Compromise, in short, does not heal the rift between the two aims. It can hide it for a while, but it will become salient enough sooner or later. A noteworthy feature of this 'solution' is that it does nothing to challenge, or to help the pupil to challenge, existing socio-economic arrangements. These are taken as read, even if attempts are made to square them with pupil-centred demands. The kinds of curricula which the compromise solution lends itself to show this clearly. The typical *primary*-school recipe of basic skills, conventional social morality and 'the much broader educational front, including art, music, movement, drama and so on', includes little that can begin to equip children with the tools of social criticism. This is evident from the recent HMI survey of

Primary Education in England (HMSO, 1978), which draws attention to the schools' general failure to teach children to argue a case, to reason things out. History and geography, both of them subjects which can help one to understand the kind of industrial society one lives in, are particularly ill-provided for. Political education is presumably so little in evidence in any of the schools surveyed that it is not mentioned even once. Those *secondary* schools which tread the path of compromise are also short on socio-economic understanding, as witnessed, for instance, by the Hansard Society's recent revelation of political ignorance among pupils in this age group (Stradling, 1977).[1]

Can anything be put in place of the compromise solution? Can one reconcile personal well-being and economic needs in any other way? Could one do it not by tampering with the concept of personal well-being so as to make it fit the *status quo*, but by critically reassessing what our economic needs are, so as to bring them closer to the requirements of personal fulfilment? If we abstract sufficiently from present realities there are some easy solutions: that machines take over from men a lot of the work that men don't want to do; that working hours are decimated in the unattractive jobs that remain; that present authoritarian patterns of dominance and submission are replaced by participatory work-place democracy. But this only shows that reconciliation between the two educational aims is possible in a society whose work arrangements are radically transformed in these ways. We are still left with the problem of what we do in *this* society.

How far could we get by making pupils critically aware of present economic realities and of the clash between these and personal requirements? It would not be difficult, I think, to engage them in discussions about possible reconciliations along the lines just suggested to do with automation, shorter working hours and work-place democracy. This would make the conflict more obvious to them, but it might also mean that they became more vociferous in pressing for these reforms to be implemented as soon as possible. If they could come about within years rather than decades, the reconciliation could happen soon enough to make it personally applicable to them. Even if it took far longer, they could still try to reconcile the two aims by doing what limited work they could to reform the system, e.g. through political action, meanwhile identifying themselves with those in future generations who would be living in a reconciled society.

There will be three sorts of objection to this proposal: that it will help to undermine or sabotage the existing economy; that it expects too much of human nature to be so self-sacrificing; and that the idea of a final reconciliation is a utopian dream.

It will certainly undermine any existing economic system which treats workers as units of labour rather than as ends-in-themselves, but that does not mean that it will make *any* form of economy unworkable. There is no reason why the present economic system should be taken as sacrosanct.

Whether it expects too much of human nature depends on *how great* the conflict is. If one is obliged to work sixteen hours a day, is debarred from trade union or other political activity and kept at near-starvation level, then it is indeed difficult to see what one can do. But in a society where one works eight or nine hours a day, can engage in political activity and is paid above the level of mere subsistence, such a reconciliation is more possible. To some extent one is able to lead a life of one's own; and where one cannot, one can identify the well-being of later workers with one's own, the more easily the nearer the future reconciliation appears to one to be. To be sure, this depends on adopting altruistic attitudes to some extent, even though altruism here coincides with one's own enlarged conception of one's well-being. And this might have implications for educational aims, since the altruism would have to be somehow acquired. But since at this point we move into the *moral* aims of education, I will postpone further discussion of the issue until after we have looked at moral aims in more detail.

Is it utopian to look forward to a final reconciliation between personal and economic aims? This depends, I think, on how high one is pitching one's demands. If one pitches them very high, it is unlikely fully to be achieved, for that would mean a society in which there was *no friction at all* between the demands of personal well-being and the demands of work. But restricting ourselves for a moment only to the sphere of personal well-being, as we saw in the last chapter conflict between our desires is ineradicable. We accept it as part of our nature, devising ways, through reflective integration, of ordering our desires so as to contain – but not to eradicate – the conflict. If we do not demand absence of all conflict in the personal sphere, why should we demand it between that sphere and the sphere of work? The more realistic kind of reconciliation is one in which, although there may still be conflict, it is not so great as to rule out, for any individual, his being able autonomously to work out his own plan of life as outlined in the last chapter.

This whole line of thought, then, rejects the 'compromise' solution and finds a reconciliation by making the economic aim subordinate to the demands of personal well-being. But it is not at all clear that we still remain totally in the sphere of *pupil-centred* aims, since the reconcilation may well involve a certain amount of self-sacrifice on at least some people's part. At this point we may conveniently turn to the moral aims of education.

Moral aims and pupil-centred aims

Introduction
A second reason why virtually everyone would object to a purely pupil-centred education is that this would take no account of moral obligations. If educators aim only at promoting the child's well-being, then the child himself may grow up thinking this is all-important. He may, for all we have said so far, grow up a complete amoralist, lacking either any understanding of moral obligations or any willingness to fulfil them. Virtually everyone will agree that education should to some extent seek to make children sensitive to the rights and interests of others, disposed to keep their promises, not to tell lies, not to injure people, to help them in distress. Problems arise once one begins pinning down the content of morality more firmly than this, since there will be wide differences of opinion about what morality does or does not involve. But it will do for the present if we accept a minimum account like this, with which few are likely to disagree.

I should make it clear at this point that I am simply taking it as read, here and henceforth, that it will not do to let a child grow up as a complete amoralist. There are no *compelling* reasons we can give him why he should be moral. We may appeal to the interests of those adversely affected by him if he is not. But unless he *cares* about those interests this is likely to fall on deaf ears. Many philosophers have argued that amoralism is irrational, that any rational man will want to be morally virtuous. As far as I can see, rational amoralism is a coherent position to adopt.[2] If anyone objects to the arguments in this and the following chapter on the grounds that an amoralist need take no notice of them, I have no answer to him. I am simply taking it for granted, as I say, that my readers, like myself, want children to be brought up with some concern for others as well as for themselves and their own projects.

Given this, we now face two problems. (a) What overall moral aims should educators have in view of the wide differences of opinion just mentioned? Is there anything like an objective position one can take up here which will deflect the usual charges that one is arbitrarily imposing on pupils one's own subjective moral beliefs? (b) How are moral aims to be related to pupil-centred and to economic aims?

We shall be able to get a clearer view of (a) via a discussion of (b). I shall begin with the relation between moral and pupil-centred aims.

We saw in the last chapter how, although moral aims are not neglected, pupil-centred aims tend now to be dominant in both educational theory and educational practice.

How does this happen in educational theory? And what relations do theorists see between the two sorts of aim? A theme which runs through both 'progressive', biologically oriented, theories and anti-progressive theories, is that moral development[3] is *a part* of personal development. In the progressives this is embedded in a theory of *instincts*. We are born with all kinds of instincts – to explore the world, for instance, to play, to construct. Among these instincts is the social or gregarious instinct. The aim of education is the full flowering of these instincts, the social instinct included. Among the critics of progressivism, some of the most influential have seen education as consisting centrally in enabling pupils to enter into a number of distinct kinds of knowledge or '*forms of understanding*'. We are not born with an aesthetic understanding, mathematical understanding, philosophical or scientific understanding, and so on: they are cultural products into which we have to be deliberately inducted. Among these forms of understanding is moral understanding. A central aim of education is to initiate pupils into all the varied forms of understanding, moral understanding included.

In both types of theory, therefore, moral learning or moral development, as just described, is just one of the elements of personal development as a whole, *on a par with* elements of other kinds.

But how are moral and pupil-centred aims related? We come back to the original question. How *can* moral learning (or development) be a part of an overall self-oriented development in view of the familiar fact that desire for one's own good and one's obligations towards others can often tug one in opposite directions?

The progressives tended to solve the problem by denying that there is any real conflict here: one comes to see that one's own good is to be identified with the good of all; so that education for individuality is at the same time education for the common good. Take, for instance, Percy Nunn: 'As the pupil's moral insight deepens, he comes to see that, while the end of moral activity is always individual good, that good can be realised only if it is identified with a universal good' (Nunn, 1920, p. 244). Moral aims need not be stressed particularly in such a theory, because they are already included within the master aim of the cultivation of individuality.

I shall return to this solution a little later on.

How do the non-progressives who rest their educational theories on 'forms of understanding' relate moral and pupil-centred aims? The general answer is: not very well. This comes out in different ways.

Sometimes moral understanding is seen, as in Hirst's theory, as constituting one of the six or seven forms of understanding which a 'liberal education' is to develop (Hirst, 1965). A 'liberal education' is not seen as the *whole* of education, only a central part of it concerned with knowledge for its own sake. Education, Hirst argues, can include other things — like physical education, for instance, or (and this is the important point) the formation of moral character. So there are two sorts of moral aim: the promotion of moral understanding for its own sake, and the formation of moral character. The second of these includes the building up of moral *dispositions*: it is not simply an intellectual matter. It should be clear that a morally good person is one who possesses, among other things, such dispositions. He has not merely, if at all, a theoretical understanding of the nature of moral rules, principles or virtues: he is inclined through habituation to *follow* these rules and principles and he actually *has* the virtues. A 'liberally educated' man in this context is not necessarily a morally good man. His interest in morality may stop at the theory of it. So the question arises; how does one relate the aim of promoting moral understanding in the theoretical way to the aim of developing morally virtuous dispositions? To this the theory of a liberal education based on the forms of understanding gives no answer, since what happens in that part of 'education' lying outside 'liberal education' is also outside the theory.

I have been assuming in this that the forms of understanding theory is 'pupil-centred', in that the development of one's intellect for its own sake is seen as a good for that person. A more explicitly pupil-centred version of the 'forms of understanding' position is that which sees these as necessary for personal autonomy. Dearden, who holds this view, does not neglect the dispositional side of moral learning, devoting a large part of a chapter to it in his *Philosophy of Primary Education* (Dearden, 1968, ch. 8). But he still faces the problem of relating his main pupil-centred aim, personal autonomy, to this moral aim. *This* moral aim is not included under personal autonomy, since once again, this embraces only understanding. The personally autonomous person is one who must have an understanding of morality, to be sure, but there is no guarantee that he will apply this understanding to virtuous ends. If he is astute, he might use it, indeed, to further his own self-centred designs: through knowing what motivates genuinely moral men and how they think about moral matters, he might be able to manipulate them all the better to his own advantage. I should stress again that Dearden thinks that education should do better than this, that it should develop moral dispositions as well. But the central point is that this recommendation comes *from outside* his main theory about personal autonomy based on the forms of understanding. So the question of how this pupil-oriented aim is to be related to the moral aim is left unresolved. We don't know, for instance, whether it would be more important, equally important, or less important. The theory does not help us.

A third variant of the non-progressive case is found in Downie, Loudfoot and Telfer (1974). In their case the problem is even more acute. Having defined 'being educated' in terms of the acquisition of knowledge alone (this is not 'forms of knowledge or understanding' in Hirst's sense), 'moral education' as this is normally understood, i.e. as including the formation of character as well as more purely intellectual achievements, becomes a kind of *contradiction in terms*. Like Dearden, these authors obviously still attach some importance to moral aims as such: they have a section in their book on 'moral education' in the familiar sense (*op. cit.*, pp. 82 ff.). But, again, their failure to notice the discrepancy means that they bypass the crucial question of *priorities* between moral and pupil-centred aims.

One move theoretically open to all these non-progressives, but a move which none of them is prepared to make, is to argue, as Socrates did, that to know the good is to do the good, i.e. that an understanding of morality brings with it dispositions to act in accordance with it. Each of the three theories could then *include* the dispositional moral aim within its framework.

It is not surprising, though, that none of the theories takes up this option. Even though it is perhaps normally true that a person who knows that he ought not to be unkind to others, for instance, is also disposed not to be unkind, it is not invariably true: he may lack the strength of will to adhere to the principles he knows are right; or he may, as already stated, use his moral knowledge for evil purposes.

The three non-progressive theories highlight aims to do with the pupil's own well-being – his being autonomous or possessing a developed intellect. The moral aim (I shall use this term henceforth to mean the formation of a morally virtuous character) is not exactly subordinated, nor exactly neglected, for it is neither; but it does not, at the very least, have the same centrality in any of the theories as pupil-centred aims. Since progressivists, too, have pressed for pupil-centred aims and are able to bring the moral aim in tow via the doctrine of the identity of individual and common good, we see that two influential schools of educational thought are allied in the lack of centrality they accord to moral aims.

Both schools of thought have influenced educational practice. We saw in the last chapter how dominant pupil-centred aims have been, not only among theorists but also among parents and teachers. Just why this should be so is a historical/sociological question of great interest, to which some sociologists of education are now beginning to turn their attention (Hargreaves, 1980). That the propagation of pupil-centred educational theories via teacher-training institutions and in other ways has helped to promote pupil-centred educational practice is undeniable. To what extent it has been an *independent* influence is another question. It *might* be that it has helped, along with, for example, parental pressures for pupil-centred ends, to push schools further in this direction. But it might also be that pupil-centred educational theory is only a *reflection* of individualistic tendencies already found in social life, i.e. that the theory only legitimates what is already happening. Certainly in what they highlight and what they lowlight the theorists are not so far removed from many a parent, quite untouched by educational theory, who wants the school to do the best by his child, equipping him to hold down a good job, make good use of his leisure etc. etc., while at the same time (this is not exactly subordinated, not exactly neglected) turning him out a decent member of society.

The common good

Of considerable interest though these speculations about causal lines of influence are, I must leave them on one side and come back to the problem of how pupil-centred and moral aims are properly to be related.

An excessively simple-minded answer would be that if the parents and teachers who educate any particular child aim at his good alone, then ideally, if every child is educated in this way, the good of each will be promoted. The education system taken as a whole, including home as well as school, has in mind, therefore, not only *this* child's well-being, but that of all others as well.

The problem with this, which has not seemed so obvious in practice as it seems on analytical inspection, is that it provides no guarantee against creating a society of completely self-centred persons. If the whole of each pupil's education is directed to his well-being, is it not *likely*, in fact, that he will come to see that well-being as supremely important?

As already stated, few would wish to stick to a *purely* pupil-centred position through thick and thin. Most pupil-centred supporters would find a place for 'moral education' as a corrective to the possibility of extreme self-involvement. It is not enough, they would argue, that *the education system* is attentive to others' interests: the *pupil himself* must be so attentive, at least to some extent.

A second, rather different, answer is the one we have already seen in progressivism, that we can still concentrate wholly on pupil-centred aims, because the pupil's good coincides with the common, or general, good. On this view there is no danger that the more each pupil pursues his own interests the more a completely self-centred society is likely to emerge, since to pursue one's own good *is* to pursue the good of all. (At the same time, we could equally well put the aim the other way round – i.e. that the pupil should strenuously work only for the common good since apparent 'self-sacrifice' of this kind is really self-fulfilment. So the aim is compatible with both a highly individualistic and a highly collectivist form of education, since each could boil down to the same thing.)

This theory provides a very neat way of solving our problem and one which has particularly appealed to religious educators who believe that the individual's good coincides with the total well-being of God's creation. It has influenced British education first *via* British idealist philosophy which flourished between 1870 and World War One and later, as we saw above, *via* Percy Nunn (Gordon and White, 1979. ch. 12).

Is it true?

If it is, then it has to cope with what is normally taken to be *conflict* between the well-being of one individual, and that of another. Suppose there is just one place in the last lifeboat after a shipwreck and the last two men on board both want it. It seems to be in both their interests to take the place, but if one gets it the other must drown. Where is the common good here?

Only two individuals are involved here and the situation is an unusual one. To take something closer to home. It may well be a part of one's well-being in the industrialised northern hemisphere to have a life-style which depends on using such a proportion of the world's resources that millions in the poorer southern hemisphere have to live below subsistence levels. On a common-good theory there could be no *real* clash at the level of individuals' well-being. It would have to say, as in the lifeboat case, that the conflict is only *apparent*, that what we uncritically take to be the good of the individual is often not his good, and that if we really knew what that good consisted in we should see that it was coincident with the common good.

How viable is this conception? We should remember that we are talking of a common good not in the instrumental way in which drains, laws, armies and roads are in the interests of all of us, but as something of intrinsic value. Can there be such a thing? What would it be like?

One candidate might be the well-being, as defined in chapter 3, of a group of individuals. But if this is not some supra-personal well-being, but the combined well-being of all members of the group, there is a problem. For each member, it seems, one can distinguish between his own well-being, as in the last sentence, and the common good, which is the combined well-being of all. So it looks as if a part of the whole must be identical with the whole.

Is this impossible? Take the situation within a typical family. The parents care for each other and they care for their children. For each of them the well-being of every other member of the family is bound up in his own: his own well-being is diminished as the well-being of others is diminished. One's own good, therefore, can expand to include others' within itself. If the others do likewise, the result is a shared, or common well-being.

But the fact that this expansion of the self *can* take place does not imply that it *must* take place. So an individual's good is not necessarily identical with a shared good: the individual may prefer to keep himself very much to himself. Educationally this is important because we still have no reason to think that by following purely pupil-centred aims one will necessarily be promoting a more general well-being.

Could such a reason be built on the social nature of man? There are good grounds for holding that individuals are not atomic entities out of which society is somehow (how?) constructed, but are essentially social beings. This conclusion could be reached empirically by observation of the kind of animal the human being is, but it has also been argued for *a priori*, by reflection on the nature of conceptual schemes: if men are, whatever else they are, concept-users and if concept-learning requires one to understand socially agreed criteria for concept-application, then men must be members of a society. Without going into further explanation or discussion of this argument, we need to ask what bearing it has on the topic of the common good. It is this. If a man could not possibly be an atomic entity, a completely private individual bound by no links to others, then how is it possible for him to have a completely privatised well-being? Since he is a social creature, must not his good expand beyond the frontiers of himself to embrace the well-being of others with whom he is connected?

But there is a telling objection to all this. The most that the point about the intersubjective nature of conceptual schemes shows is that, *in order to become* an individual, one has to have been brought up in a society. It does not follow from this that, having become an individual, one cannot turn into the most self-centred of egoists. Of course, such an egoist can always be mistaken about his good, believing it to reside in the self-centred concerns, whereas in fact it lies elsewhere. But the important point is that individual good *may* be located where the egoist thinks it is: we cannot conclude that the individual good which a socialised individual follows *must* be a common good, without begging the question.

But the anti-social egoist, it may be argued, must surely be an exception. It is true that individuals cannot become what they are without being brought up within a shared form of life. But the point about the social nature of man goes further than this. Humanity could not exist at all if *everyone* were an anti-social egoist. It must be normally the case that individuals value their links with the society which has contributed so much to making them what they are. Normally, then, they must seek to foster the well-being of society, not concentrating wholly on what they take to be a private, non-social, well-being of their own.

There are many difficulties in this line of thought, but the one most pertinent to us is that, even granted that the anti-social individual must be an exception, it has not been shown either that the normal individual's well-being must coincide with the well-being of society, or that the latter must be a *common* well-being. For his interest in the general social well-being may be nothing more than a reflection of a *moral* obligation laid upon him: as a moral agent, he has a duty to consider the good of all, not only his own good. If this is so, his pursuit of his own good may be straightforwardly at odds with his moral duty, so there is no necessary coincidence between his own and the general good. Neither is it necessary that the general good be a *common* good: if morality enjoins him to consider the good of all, this good may still fray into the separate individual goods of the different members of the society.

The upshot of the argument from the social nature of man seems to be that it is too weak to show that there must be a common good. Is the religious conception of it any more convincing? An individual's well-being is now identical, so it is claimed, with a larger good, the well-being of the whole of God's created universe, or perhaps of God himself. Whichever it is, this type of common good theory obviously assumes the existence not only of God but also of this larger, divine good. None but the most bigoted could claim that these assumptions are so well-founded that educators are justified in imposing on children a set of aims that presupposes them – in urging them to think that their own well-being consists in this larger good. It is one thing to hold this belief oneself, but quite another to inculcate it in others, with or without a surrounding web of 'justifications'. Religiously minded educators of this sort should have a heavy conscience. What if they are wrong and human good lies not in the fulfilment of a mythical divine will, but in the satisfaction of man's 'animal' desires as extended by culture along the lines of the discussion in chapter 3? They might have spent their lives misleading generations of pupils about their good: no small mistake. How, in any case, are pupils to know what this mysterious larger good consists in? By what can they direct their lives? Must they simply have faith, trust the wisdom of authorities? Is faith the answer, too, for their teachers when they begin to wonder whether they are doing the right thing? A lot of religious people will say that it is. But this is really a very odd move to make. As one's doubts about something one believes increase, one has more and more reason to relinquish one's belief, not to hold on to it all the more fervently in the teeth of the opposition.

I realise that this will cut no ice with many religious people. 'What's so good about reason?' some might say. 'All this just begs the question against the superiority of faith.' The arguments and objections could go on and on. But I propose to stop them here, taking it that the religious version of the common good rests on too many doubtful assumptions to make any but the least rational of religious educators unhappy to incorporate it into their picture of education and its aims if this means steering children into accepting it.

If individual and common good cannot be shown to coincide, what other kind of relations could there be between pupil-centred and moral aims? This is not at all a merely academic question. Both aims are found, to differing extents in most, if not all, schools; pupils come under their guidance; and if their teachers do not have a clear understanding of how they are to be related, what hope have *they* of making sense of it all? If 90 per cent of, say, a 14-year-old's time is taken up with CSE or GCE courses whose most obvious rationale is to improve his own chances of a 'good job' or access to higher education, what attitude is he to take to the moral education which the school provides for him either as a curriculum subject or in more informal ways? Which is to be more important to him – the upward struggle for self-advancement or attention to the needs of others as well as himself? If so very much of his time at school is officially programmed for his self-advancement, and if not only his teachers but also his parents want him to 'better himself', is he not likely to be inclined, finally, in the egocentric direction? But the school still presents his moral obligations as important to him, perhaps as overridingly so. How can he square the two contradictory demands? There are several possible outcomes. He may settle for a trimmed down version of morality which he can make as compatible as possible with his self-centred ambitions. This will be all the easier if he can represent these ambitions to himself in a moralised light: if, for instance, he can conceptualise the acting career on which he has set his heart as publicly beneficial. But psychological tension will persist in so far as this compatibility is incomplete. In other cases, the individual may incorporate both the moral demands of the one part of his schooling and the self-centred pressures of the other, without becoming aware of their incompatibility. This may obviate the psychological stress, but may also lead to the kind of character-inadequacy which E. M. Forster portrayed in the person of Henry Wilcox in *Howard's End*, the failure of a man to *connect* his different motives and attitudes, to become conscious of their mutual contradictions. A third way of removing the tension might be to decide to sacrifice all personal ambitions in favour of the altruistic duties which one's moral education appears to demand of one. But there is something desperate about this manoeuvre. Can one *really* be doing what is morally right if one embraces morality as a means of avoiding personal stress? Can one excise egocentric ends from one's life *completely*?

An empirical study of how pupils cope with this tension would be of great interest. But to return to our main problem: what guidance can teachers be given in helping pupils to cope? How can the twin aims be reconciled?

The minimalist view

I said just now that a pupil could opt for a 'trimmed-down' version of morality which he could square with his private ambitions. This might be the most reasonable thing to do in any case. For in so far as they make moral prescriptions at all, schools may often be too demanding. Stories of saintliness or items about world poverty in school assemblies may lead some children to think that if they were *really* good they should sacrifice their own happiness completely for the sake of others. Christianity, which in many of its forms shares this point of view with secular moralities based on utilitarian or Kantian principles, is often a powerful influence on the ethos of the school and may well help to reinforce this reaction. But behind this official, very stringent outlook one often finds a more relaxed, more 'realistic' understanding of the moral life. This percolates into the school from the wider society and guides the actual behaviour of pupils and staff alike to different degrees regardless of what lip-service they may pay to the official line. It would be more honest, and it might well make for less confusion of thought, if schools got rid of this double standard and encouraged the more realistic version of morality which could lock nicely with their pupil-centred aims.

So, at least, one might argue. What would this realistic morality contain and what might be said in its defence?

The sketch might go something like this. For each person his own well-being is of central importance in his life. It is in his, as in everyone else's interests, if there are generally accepted moral rules providing a framework of security within which people can pursue their own ends, i.e. without the constant fear that they will be physically harmed, cheated, deceived, bullied or in other ways done down: unless men generally keep their promises, tolerate others' opinions, are fair in their dealings with them, life becomes unbearable for all.

It is a logical part of such a moral theory that the moral demands made on the individual should be kept down to a minimum. The more such demands encroach on his time and attention, the less opportunity he has to pursue his own good. Obviously they could never be reduced to zero; but the ideal society will make them as little irksome as possible. They will be least irksome where the demands on the individual are mainly of a negative sort – not to injure others, deceive them, impose one's will on them, and so on. Duties like these, being negative, take no time to fulfil and make no demands on private resources; fulfilling them, therefore, need not deflect one at all from private ambitions. Duties of active benevolence, though, are a different matter. Benevolence *does* take time and often involves material costs: the more one helps others to realise their ends, the less time and possibly money etc., one has to devote to one's own, so there is a very real conflict here. One would expect the moral theory under discussion, therefore, to play down the obligation of active benevolence. The ideal society will be one in which each individual does not *need* others' help, but is quite able to stand on his own feet. No doubt there will be occasions where individuals cannot help themselves, and where the duty of benevolence must come to the fore; but it should be social policy to keep these occasions to a minimum.

The minimalist morality I have been sketching is recognisably one of the several main theoretical determinants in contemporary politics, though its adherents will not all hold it in the pure form stated here. Its influence is found not least in the educational system, where it helps to provide a rationale for the practice of aiming *primarily* at the well-being of one's pupils, while ensuring that they acquire certain minimal moral dispositions.

In this latter conception of education we find a possible answer to our question how pupil-oriented and morally-oriented aims are to be related to each other. To many it will seem the only sensible answer: within a minimum framework of moral rules individuals should be encouraged to live for their own private ends; and schools should fit their pupils for a predominantly individualistic society of this sort.

The answer reflects a widely held belief about how we should lead our lives. It does not advocate, it is worth noting, an out-and-out egoism once the minimal moral demands are met. It is not saying that within the area of his own ends the individual should live only for himself. It would be unusual, in fact, if he did so. As we saw when discussing the common good theory, people can expand their notion of well-being to embrace that of family or friends; men, being the social creatures they are, may normally be expected to do this. If for some reason they do not, that is up to them. Provided he fulfils his moral obligations, a man can live alone on an island, literally or metaphorically. But he is likely to be a rarity.

So despite what I seemed to be saying above, minimalist morality does not try to reduce all benevolence to a minimum. What it *does* reduce is the *moral obligation* of benevolence. A man may be as attentive as he pleases to the well-being of his friends and relatives, where the benevolence is unconstrained, not obliged; it flows towards the fulfilment of his own desires.

While not narrowly egoistical, the minimalist morality does claim to take a realistic view of the place of self-interest in human life. Christian or secular moralities which put all the emphasis on universal love take too little regard of human nature. It is not within the powers of the normal person to be so altruistic. We are so constituted as to put ourselves at the centre of things. Saints may break free, but saints are rare. Education could in principle help turn us all into saints but only at the cost of tampering with human nature as we know it. We might all be brainwashable into altruists. But at what cost? And what right would the brainwashers have to change our natures?

This, then, is the minimalist morality. It is the morality appropriate to a capitalist society, with its belief in the pursuit of private profit within a framework of basic moral rules and it is the kind of morality which can support the pre-eminence of pupil-centred aims in education. It is reasonable, does not demand more than human nature can allow, and is flexible enough to allow people to occupy themselves with others' interests as much as they wish.

But will it do?

One thing that is still not clear is how extensive its moral obligations go. There are no problems over rules to do with promise-keeping, non-injury, truth-telling. These are so obviously necessary for any tolerable social life that they must be included in any minimal framework. (As with any moral rule, there is no need to insist that one keeps one's promises, tells the truth etc. in *any* circumstances. I am taking it as read here that every moral rule is only prima facie obligatory, that is, that it can always be overridden by another moral rule which has higher priority in the circumstances.) But what about benevolence? It has not been ruled out as a moral obligation, although its sphere has been circumscribed. But how circumscribed should it be? What is the minimum which the minimalist morality will allow in this area?

I was looking this morning at an old copy of *The Times* for 1856. Several rich people were advertising for servants of all kinds, offering them £10 or £15 per annum plus board. That there were plenty of takers for such jobs was evident from the 'Situations wanted' on another page. Now it is quite likely that an employer of that time offering £40 or £50 per annum because he thought one could not lead a decent human life on less would have been labelled by his peers as either mad or preternaturally saintly. But *would* he have been saintly? Or from our vantage point over a century later do we say that what he did was only what could be morally expected of him?

How does the minimal moralist decide where to draw the line when it comes to actively promoting others' well-being? Should one do what is conventionally acceptable? But today's conventions may be unacceptable tomorrow. Might one then be seen as doing less than he ought? What special authority, in any case, have the standards of one's own age?

Can the moralist work out rationally, without undue regard for conventional expectations, what his minimal obligations are? If he sees a child hit by a passing car, should he go to his aid? Both convention and 'common humanity' would say 'yes'. If a starving man comes up to him and asks him for the price of a loaf of bread, should he refuse? This sort of thing does not happen in our kind of society today, so convention does not pronounce on the matter, but, if it did happen, only a moral monster could urge him to look the other way. What, now, about starving masses overseas? Has he any minimal obligation to help in their relief, either by voluntary contributions, for instance, or by voting for government action on their behalf?

If the answer is 'no', then what makes this case different from the case of the starving man in the street? Is being *face to face* with others' distress the crucial factor? But why should this be relevant? It is certainly more difficult to escape moral blame for letting a starving man die on your doorstep than for letting unknown thousands die in Africa or Asia, but to make *this* the ground of distinction is to show that one's real commitments are not moral ones, after all, but prudential: one is less interested in doing what is morally right than in preserving one's moral reputation. More generally, if we have *no* moral obligations towards the world's starving, then where does the obligation of benevolence stop? The difficulty is that wherever one might say it stopped would have an *arbitrary* air about it, whether one drew the line to enclose only those with whom one was in face-to-face contact, or members of one's nation, or one's 'kith-and-kin', or one's 'race', or whomever. The one sure way of getting over the problem is to deny that there is *any* moral obligation of benevolence at all. Whether and in what ways he is benevolent is to be left to the individual himself. He is likely, coming from a sociable species, to be naturally interested in the welfare of others, not only his family and friends but also, on occasion, strangers like the starving man or the injured boy, whose distress moves him to sympathy and to action on their behalf. He may or may not feel sympathetic to more distant suffering: if he does, he may well act; if he does not, he is not to be blamed. This line of thought would cut the obligation of benevolence out of morality, reducing the latter to such areas as keeping one's word, telling the truth, honesty, refraining from injuring or killing people, and so on. And *then* the questions would be: why circumscribe morality at that point, rather than building in benevolence? And again: are we still talking about *morality* if we write out of it any obligation to attend to others' welfare? What distinguishes the person who takes this line from the pure egoist? Is it that the moral man, unlike the egoist, keeps his word etc. even when it is not in his interest to do so? But *why* does he keep his word? If he does it out of concern for others, he is following some kind of moral principle of benevolence. This can't be the reason in this case, however, since we are currently writing such a principle out of morality. But if he is not doing it for self-interested reasons either, then why is he doing it? If he has no reason, he is acting irrationally.

I shall come back in a moment to the general problem of moral motivation. So far I have been looking at the view that one has *no* moral obligation to help the world's starving. I don't know how many minimal moralists, if asked, *would* take this line, but I suspect that many, if not most, would accept *some* moral responsibility here. Even the most egocentric of Western governments, for instance, give *some* overseas aid to poor countries, although the amount is often small; and presumably those who vote them into office think this is a good thing to do. Given that the minimal moralist accepts this responsibility, how far does it go? How much help should he give? Peter Singer has suggested that those living in richer countries should give all their income except what is necessary for their basic needs (Singer, 1979). Is this about right? The minimal moralist is hardly likely to agree. He might be prepared for a few pennies of his income tax to be directed into aid programmes and he might put a few more pennies in Oxfam collecting boxes, but giving up several hundred or possibly thousand pounds per annum would be out of the question: heroic moral gestures are for moral heroes, not for the ordinary man. Where, then, does he draw the line? And why does he draw it there? Why are a few pence an acceptable sacrifice but not a few hundred pounds? A plausible answer is that a few pence are not enough to hurt one's own pocket, but just about enough, when aggregated in a national budget, to make it appear to others that one, or one's nation, is doing what is morally right for the world's poor. If this is the reason, once again it is a prudential one, not a moral one. If he stays, however, within the moral sphere, the minimal moralist still has to say what will be the extent of his beneficence and why, if it falls short of Singer's stringent demand, he stops it, or lets it run thin, at this point rather than that. Can he give a non-arbitrary answer which is not a mere rationalisation of an underlying self-concern? How much altruism can he accept while still sticking to his basic belief that his own interests should be central? This belief, which is the basic rationale for his minimalism, must constantly steer him towards restrictiveness. But how is he to justify making the restriction he does, in *moral* terms? He may be able to justify it, as we have seen, by reference to self-interest, but then benevolence ceases to be a *moral* principle. If his justification refers to others' interests, not only his own, then why cut things short here rather than there? Why should *these* people be worthy of support and not those? How can arbitrariness be avoided?

I mentioned just above the wider topic of moral motivation. This applies to the minimalist's whole morality, not only to benevolence. Why does he believe that he should keep his promises, abstain from injury etc. as well as be benevolent? We have seen that at a general level he thinks moral rules in these areas are a necessary condition of a society where each individual is maximally free to go about his own business. But while this provides him with a reason for insisting that these rules are *generally* obeyed, it does not go so far as to show why *everyone* must obey them. If a few people cut corners there will be little effect on the whole: the desired sort of society will still be realisable. Is there any reason why *he* shouldn't be one of these corner-cutters or free-riders? Suppose he has made a promise that he finds irksome to keep. Has he any good reason to keep it? He has justified morality at a general level in terms of the self-interest of individuals. In particular, it is in his own interest that moral rules are generally respected. But if his own well-being is his principal lodestar, why not follow it when it comes to breaking or keeping an awkward promise? One reason which might weigh with him is his reputation: if he breaks his promise, people will be less likely to trust him in future, so he has good grounds for keeping it. This is a prudential reason, as it appeals, once again, to his own interests. But suppose he is able to cheat or deceive and get away with it. What should he do then? Suppose, for instance, that he can doctor his income-tax returns to his own advantage, knowing that the likelihood of his being found out is zero or nearly zero. Should he or should he not deceive the Inland Revenue? I cannot see that the minimal moralist has any reason for being honest. Self-interest is his principal motive; as long as people are generally honest the kind of society he wants will be a reality; so why should he not be a free-rider? He may, it is true, resist the temptation. He may 'stick to his principles' in an upright kind of way. But then why should he do so? It is not a self-evident truth that one ought to keep one's promises or refrain from lying or stealing. If he is a rational man, he will have to provide a reason. But within his own framework of assumptions there is no obvious reason that he can give. He can stick to his principles despite that, of course, but then he begins to look irrational, perhaps the sort of man who has had it drummed into him in childhood that he ought not to do this or that and has always taken this as read without reflection.

So the choices for the minimal moralist seem to be irrational rule-worship on the one hand or free-riding on the other. The second of these takes him out of the moral sphere altogether. He may *appear* to others to act morally, since it is in his interests to keep his word etc. most of the time, but his guiding principle both when he toes the moral line and when he cuts his moral corners is always his own good. Underneath he is nothing more than an egoist.

Minimal moralism is an influential force in the world we live in. It produces variants of both the character-types just distinguished, the rule-bound and the egoistical. It would require empirical research to see which of these was more widespread, but it is clear enough from one's own experience that egoistic attitudes are not uncommon, and not only in the veiled form described so far. Tax-dodging, for instance, is not by any means something which individuals keep quiet about so that their moral reputation is unimpugned. Quite the contrary. People openly discuss ways of doing it, even boast about doing it; domestic plumbers and electricians make no secret of why they would rather be paid in cash; if you say that you think everyone should declare everything and that you intend to do so yourself, you are made to feel a prig or an idiot. (Granted, all this ignores the non-egoistic reasons some people have for not paying taxes – antipathy to government spending on defence, for instance.) We live in a society in which the egoist has less and less need to be hypocritical, to cloak himself in outward respectability as he had to two or three generations back. Selfish motives are now so commonly avowed that he loses less than he used to by avowing them himself. Reputation comes from conforming to others' expectations of one; so if people are expected to be selfish, he has often more to gain by being so openly than by being so by stealth.

I am not claiming that this new frankness about one's motives applies to all areas of contemporary morality. Perhaps one should see tax-dodging as something which has, as it were, been cut away, for many people, from the sphere of morality: they may genuinely abhor dishonesty but just not see, or keep themselves from seeing, that the way they fill in their tax returns falls under that heading.

I should make it clear, again, that I do not want to exaggerate the extent of selfish motivation in our society: I don't have the overall facts and am only recording my own impressions of one general attitude among many. But as part of the social ethos, egoism can be expected to affect the outlooks of those being educated, both in school and out of it. This raises the questions, to which I shall return, to what extent should it or any other morally relevant attitude be encouraged? To what extent should it be controlled, its influence limited?

Before I finish this discussion of minimalism and link it up with the main theme of this chapter, let me try to get further to grips with the basic assumption embedded in it. This is that for each person his own well-being is of central importance in his life: the minimum framework of moral rules subserves this overarching end. Suppose, now, we ask the minimalist for his reasons for making this assumption. 'Why is *your* well-being so important? You could have started from more altruistic assumptions: after all, there are plenty of other people around to whose interests you could have decided to devote a large part of your life. Why have you given such prominence to yourself? What is so special about you that you think you are worthy of all this self-attention?'

The appeal behind these questions is to the principle of impartiality which is found in many moral systems and, some would argue, must be found in any, if it is properly to be called a *rational* system. The principle of impartiality states that one should not make distinctions between people in the way one treats them, unless there is some relevant ground for discriminating between them. It lies at the basis, for instance, of recent legislation about racial and sexual equality: if one refuses a job to a person solely on the grounds that she is black or is a woman, this ground for discrimination is irrelevant to one's decision: blackness and femaleness are not relevant to a person's suitability as a train-driver or teacher.[4] The same principle can be applied to the minimalist: if you make your own well-being of central concern, what is relevantly different about you, as compared with other people, that justifies you in singling yourself out for special treatment?

There are two ways open for the minimalist. He may try to answer the question, or he may repudiate it. How, first, might he try to answer it?

He might argue that there *is* something special about him. He is an intellectual or artistic genius, for instance: if he fails to cosset himself, the world will be the loser. As it stands, this seems to deny the minimalist assumption that it is one's ego that is at the centre of things: the 'world' now shifts to that position. Something similar happens if he argues that, given that the overall point of morality is the promotion of the well-being of all, this general well-being will best be promoted if everyone promotes his own: once again, one's own concerns are not the ultimate *raison d'être*. If the minimalist cannot back up this new empirical claim – and it is hard to see how he could in the light of historical and other evidence that the weakest tend to go to the wall in a self-help society – then he is rationally constrained to step out of his minimalism into a more fully clothed morality which takes as its starting point the general well-being, without any egoistic preconceptions.

A third tack he might follow is that he cannot help devoting such attention to himself, because that is the way he, like the rest of us, is made. He is constitutionally incapable of being more of an altruist than this.

This is a strong argument, if true, since one cannot talk of what people ought to do except on the presupposition that they can do this. Is it true? Common experience tells us that some people are more active than others on other people's behalf. There is a gamut which we can probably all recognise in our acquaintances from very selfish individuals at one end to the very selfless at the other. If our minimalist is inclined to selfishness, how does he know that he could not be more altruistic, or have become so through his upbringing? If he argues that, because he is of the human species, he is naturally egoistical, experience seems to tell against him; and if he claims that while others may be altruists, there is something peculiar about his make-up which makes him irredeemably an egoist, then how does he know this? Has he tried to be more outward-looking but failed? Or is he rationalising his egoism without having put it to the test?

Of course in one way even the altruist will put himself in the centre of things. For he, too, if he is the self-determining agent described in the last chapter, will live according to his life-plan, pursuing *his own* (i.e. altruistic) ends resolutely, unwilling to be sidetracked on to other things. To some degree it may be true that human beings are self-concerned creatures of this sort. But this has nothing to do with the argument of the minimalist. For if minimalism means anything, it means not having to pay all but the most restricted attention to others' needs if one does not want to. When the minimalist says that men cannot be other than self-centred, he means not that they are bound to be self-determining – which in greater or lesser degree may be true – but that they cannot help being selfish; and that seems unfounded.

Neither is his case much advanced if he says that he is not claiming that men must always be selfish but, rather that their benevolence is bound to be limited. Few individuals think *only* of themselves, he may argue; most care also for their families, friends and so on, but cannot be made to extend this concern beyond this circle − except in unusual circumstances, as in times of war, for instance. Here again, what grounds can the minimalist provide for saying that sympathies are unextendable beyond a certain point? There is just so much evidence to the contrary. A couple of centuries ago and more it might well have been hard to care about the fortunes of those in other countries or even in one's own: one knew so little about them. But today when television brings us daily pictures of undernourished children in the Third World, victims of local wars or local oppression, poorly off people in our own society, it makes no sense to say that our sympathies cannot be stretched. The fact is, rather, that once we allowed them full rein, they could be stretched endlessly and in several, often conflicting, directions. It is just not true that we must remain limited altruists. (But it may well be true that it is because some of us could not face the great and conflicting demands on us which would follow if we went where our natural sympathies led us, that we draw in our moral horns and retreat into stony self-interest.)

This concludes my discussion of minimalist morality. I have spent some time on it because it is becoming an increasingly popular view. It is not only a part of the social ethos, but is also being shored up and made respectable through the writings of contemporary moral philosophers.[5] In a world short of resources where the 'laager mentality' may be expected increasingly to prevail, both between North and South and between the haves and the have-nots within any particular national community, it could well become the dominant ethic of the medium-term future.

It is likely, therefore, to become even more educationally influential than it is at present. As I said earlier, today the theory of minimal morality offers an attractive and elegant rationale for educators' practice of aiming predominantly at promoting the well-being of their pupils, while trying to ensure that they live within a minimum framework of moral rules. Its influence may well grow for the reasons mentioned.

My main concern, however, is less with what might happen in the future than with trying to work out a rationally defensible set of educational aims. I hope it should be evident by now what difficulties there are in accepting moral minimalism and the prescriptions about aims which flow from it. If we want to find a more adequate way of tying together pupil-centred and moral aims, we must look in a different direction.

Universalistic morality
We can begin from the point about impartiality raised a few paragraphs back. In considering people's interests, a rational person has, prima facie, no grounds for discriminating in favour of himself rather than others. He has good reason, therefore, to treat others as he treats himself, caring for their welfare without putting any into an unjustifiably privileged position.

We now reach something like the Christian prescription that one should love one's neighbours as oneself; or the utilitarian principle that one should work for the general happiness, each person, including oneself counting as one and no more than one; or a version of Kantianism, which emphasises a commitment to treating all men, again including oneself, as ends-in-themselves. The big differences between these philosophies matter less here than their similarity: each of them advocates some form of universal concern. A universal morality of this sort is not *completely* altruistic, in the sense that the individual lives *only* for others and not at all for himself. The rational pressure from the principle of impartiality tells against complete altruism as much as against complete egoism: what is so special about oneself that one should pay *no* attention to one's well-being while attending to everybody else's? The most rational thing to do, *ceteris paribus*, would be to follow Bentham and let each beneficiary, including oneself, count as one and no more than one.

This kind of moral outlook, especially in its Christian form, is at least as widespread in educational circles as the minimalist, probably much more so if one looks only at the official moral doctrines which parents and teachers transmit and not at the unintended influence of the general social ethos. If schools were to adopt it as a rationale for their educational aims and wanted to bring other aims in tow behind it, they would be obliged to change a good deal of their current practice. Unlike minimalism, which often fits this hand-in-glove, universalist morality would mean a radical demotion of much pupil-oriented activity and much more emphasis on curricula and forms of school organisation which encouraged the growth of this more generous moral outlook. Children might still be studying many of the same subjects as under minimalism, but in a quite different spirit: a sixth former might be doing mathematics, for instance, not because he wanted to go on to university and land a comfortable, well-paid and prestigious job, but because he wanted to become an engineer, helping to build machinery necessary for the economic infrastructure of everyone's well-being. In some countries, notably in the Communist world, a universalistic morality does power coherent sets of educational aims, at least in theory. How far should we wish our own schools, and our education system more widely, to move more consciously in this direction?

One difficulty with universalism lies in defining the 'others', all of whose interests one must consider impartially with one's own. Christianity speaks of loving one's *neighbours*, but, as we saw in discussing minimalism, there would be problems of arbitrariness if one took this in anything like a literal sense. Why should one be concerned only with those living around one? Or, more broadly, only with those with whom one is in a face-to-face relationship? There is no obvious reason why morality should be circumscribed at this point. But, equally, there seems no good reason why the moral agent should care only for those who belong to his tribe or his nation. He has just as much reason to consider the interests of those who live outside this community as of those who live within in. Is it then the good of the *world* community which he must have in mind? If it is, it cannot include only those living today, since there are no grounds for excluding the unborn. The pupil, it seems, must seek to promote the well-being of the whole of mankind, now and in the future: this can be the only moral principle which can guide him. But how could anything so immensely abstract ever be cashed in his day-to-day behaviour? How would he know where to begin? Of course, there are always *means* which he could rationally help to facilitate. If there are to be any future generations, the present generation must at least have the bare necessities of life in order to be able to bring up the next. This may provide him with a more specific injunction than that he should promote the good of all men at all times, but it is still extremely general, and there are still questions of priority as between present and future needs.

Universalistic morality is not only difficult to apply in practice. It also runs counter to a deeply held and widely shared belief in the worth of individuals and individual lives. This may seem odd in a philosophy whose interest is in the well-being of every individual without discrimination. But it follows from its drive towards as large a totality of beneficiaries as possible that any particular individual is of minimal importance. This does not mean only that because one's legitimate interest in oneself vanishes almost to zero, universalistic morality becomes virtually indistinguishable from complete altruism; but also that other individuals, too, are of negligible significance. If the good of mankind as a whole is overriding, then how could one bother about the fortunes of one's relatives or acquaintances, or, indeed, of an even larger circle? If their lot, like one's own, is a life sacrificed to the greater good, then so be it.

Universalism has been called 'the ethics of fantasy' (Mackie, 1977, p. 129). It is so impracticable and counter-intuitive that it is an impossible morality to live by. Men can and do pay lip-service to it, but their real moral commitments often lie elsewhere. Universalism has been seen as the morality of the hypocrite. This may take one form in the evangelical Christianity of Victorian England and another in the utilitarianism of contemporary Soviet Russia, but it will often tend to mask more realistic and less high-flown moral attitudes: people will show in their behaviour that they think it *is* right to work for their own good or the good of those close to them. Some may be exceptions. Dickens's Mrs Jellyby toiled for the spiritual enlightenment of the West Africans while her young children fell downstairs, went without clean clothes and got stuck in railings, all to her unconcern. But one escapes hypocrisy only at the cost of fanaticism either at the domestic or the national level.

Concrete morality
One reaction to the failure of universalism has been to preserve its unselfishness while jettisoning its unlimitedness: this has led to attempts to *localise* one's moral life within smaller-scale communities. Historically, as in Hegel and the British idealists, this has gone together with a belief in the coincidence of individual and common good (Gordon and White, 1979). The individual lives in a number of communities, each nesting inside another, from the family through neighbourhood and other local groupings to the state and thence to humanity as a whole: within each of these his well-being is identical with that of everybody else. We have already seen reasons for dismissing a common good theory. The idea of making moral obligations concrete is, nevertheless, appealing if one remembers the impracticalities of universalism. Can one construct a version of concrete morality which avoids difficulties already met elsewhere?

One might imagine the founder-members of a new small community attempting something like this. Each person within the community works for the good of all, himself included. Not only does he have to sacrifice less of his own interests than in working for the good of humanity unlimited; but he also gets more benefit, being in a smaller group of beneficiaries, from the efforts of others. In so far as the minimal moralists are right in claiming that human beings are not made for self-sacrifice beyond a certain point, their claim can be allowed. At the same time one preserves the impartiality so characteristic of universalism: each individual counts himself only as one.

But a difficulty with tailor-made communities is: what relationships are they to have with people outside them? Collective egoism now becomes an obvious threat: group members have no reason to bother about outsiders' interests if their morality ends at their own boundaries. If it is just arbitrary to end it there, they still face the universalist's challenge 'what is so special about *you*?'

The same applies if we try to work from existing communities. The family community cannot live only for itself, neither can a local community, a tribe, or a nation.

But can charity not at least *begin* at home, even though it cannot end there? What was wrong with Mrs Jellyby was that she neglected those close to her while absorbed in those far away. Whether or not she was doing good on the larger scale, she was certainly failing to do it on the smaller. This suggests that one would do well to make sure that one fulfils one's local obligations before attending to those less local. Smaller groups are not cut off from larger ones, on this view. They cannot live just for themselves. But their claims have a priority among their members: only when these are met does one go into questions of priorities *vis-à-vis* other groups.

Even this does not get us out of the wood. For suppose this latter review of priorities shows that if the small group's claims are met, other groups will suffer. Suppose, for instance, if every family in Europe saw to it that the well-being of each of its members was maximally promoted, this would mean that the poorer countries of the world would become even poorer. Would not one have to reverse engines and begin from the priorities within the larger whole, thus going straight back into universalism?

One further point about concrete morality. The idealist tradition sees smaller communities as nesting inside larger communities, rather like Russian dolls. But is there any good reason to see things this way? Individuals typically belong to a number of different groups, not all of which fit together like this. One's family and one's work-group are both part of one's state-community, but neither is nested in the other; and not all one's links with extra-state communities need be mediated via the state: one can be a member of Oxfam, for instance, or the Roman Catholic church.

Difficulties in concrete morality cast doubt on various kinds of educational aims, not only those to do with living in small self-contained communities, but also idealist conceptions of bringing children up as members of nested communities from the family through to the state and beyond.

Towards a resolution

We are still seeking an adequate relationship between pupil-centred and moral aims of education. Various suggestions have been rejected: (a) that the pupil's good is identical with the good of others; (b) that his good should be of central importance to him within a framework of minimal moral duties; (c) that he should work self-sacrificingly for the good of humanity; (d) that he should work for the good of small communities which, being small, help him to realise his own well-being and which may be nested within larger communities linking him to mankind as a whole.

The arguments so far may look purely destructive and unhelpful. But they contain the materials for a more satisfactory account.

To launch this, I want to go back to a point about the pupil's good made in chapter 3. A lot of stress was laid there on the autonomy of the individual, on his self-determination according to a life-plan embodying his own resolutions of conflicts among preferences. So far in this section on moral aims I have not said much, if anything, about autonomy. Each of the moral positions I have outlined could be held non-autonomously, that is, without the moral agent's having reflected on it and made it his own. It would be possible, for instance, to indoctrinate pupils, perhaps via Christianity, to believe that their own good coincides with a good common to humanity. Many children are indeed brought up in this way and take this coincidence as read. Vying with religious morality in our own society is ego-centred minimalism. Even more of our children (I would guess) come to accept without question the guidelines which this provides. Elsewhere in the world, in Russia, for instance, children are urged to work self-sacrificingly for the good of all − and again this is taken as a basic axiom not to be questioned. Small-scale communitarianism is equally open to indoctrination.

For some moral philosophers, Kant, for instance, being autonomous is a defining characteristic of moral agency: if one believes that one ought not to steal because one's teachers, for instance, have told one that this is wrong, one acts heteronomously, not autonomously; to act morally one must have thought through one's principles and accepted them on their own merits. Other philosophers have questioned the logical necessity of autonomy. Hegel, most notably, located the moral life, at least for most people, in *Sittlichkeit*, or the unreflective acceptance of the social ethos.

I am prepared to accept the opposition case on this matter. Anthropological investigations over the past century have shown us that other peoples, living at a sub-autonomous level, have codes of conduct which it is perfectly natural to think of as tribal moralities; and if we insisted on moral agents in our own society passing the test of reflectiveness, their numbers might be fewer than we might think. But the issue is, at root, a matter for conceptual decision and I am less interested in that just now than in relating moral and pupil-centred aims.

Even though autonomy may not be a necessary constituent of any morality, there is a good reason for including it within the moral aims of education, in the complex kind of society in which we live. I qualify things in this way because moral *conflicts* are more prominent in this sort of society than in societies of a simpler, more ritualised and less self-conscious kind. Conflict can arise in different ways. In particular situations different moral rules may prescribe different courses of action: a doctor, knowing that his patient has got incurable cancer, may be torn between telling him the truth, thus causing him misery, and saving him from anguish at the cost of telling a lie. There can be conflicts not only between rules but also between interests: as when I ask myself whether I should spend my spare income on myself, on needy relatives or on famine relief; or when doctors, again, have to choose between saving a baby or a mother. In conflict situations like these the agent cannot simply stick to the rules found in his society, for the rules do not tell him what he should do. He has to move to a more reflective level. This entails clarity about the rules and facts involved in his situation which are relevant to the judgment he will finally have to make. And judgment is inescapable here. Beyond a certain point there are no rules to guide him: he will have to weigh the different courses of action open to him and come down, taking all relevant factors into account, on one side or the other.

Conflicts do not arise at every point of one's moral life. Far from it. For the most part one knows what one should do. In these cases the autonomous moral agent will not need to reflect at every point, for he has built up a general disposition to tell the truth, keep his promises, avoid malice etc.: doing these things has become second nature to him. But there will quite frequently be times when things are not so clear-cut and he has to weigh different claims or obligations. These can occur either at the personal level, in his face to face dealings with others, or at a remoter level, in his activities as a citizen, for instance, in judging, e.g. whether more government money should be spent on defence or on the social services.

Moral autonomy in the pupil is desirable, therefore, because of the conflicts which are bound to be a feature of his moral life. The argument parallels the discussion of personal autonomy in chapter 3. There, too, the autonomous agent was faced inevitably with conflicts of inclination. The difference is that his conflicts then were between his own preferences, as related to his well-being in general, whereas now, in moral autonomy, they are between moral rules or different parties' interests, as related to his leading a morally virtuous life. In both cases the autonomous agent tries to resolve his conflicts within an integrating system of beliefs: at the personal level within a unifying plan of life and at the moral level within a coherent framework of moral rules and principles. In both cases the agent needs to have consciously thought through the system which is guiding him, trying to ensure that it is consistent, not obscure, does justice to relevant empirical facts, is adjusted as his patterns of weighting change etc.

If we go back now to the wider question of how moral aims of education are to be related to pupil-centred ones, it should at least be clear that they each embody the same kind of features: conflict, autonomous judgment in conflict situations, integrating belief-systems. But this does not take us very far. Greenland and Tasmania are related to each other in that they both share the common feature of being islands: moral and pupil-centred aims are more intimately related than that.

We are presupposing pupils who are not being brought up as thoroughgoing egoists but as good persons. Precisely what content is to be included in 'moral goodness' has not been specified, but pupils must at least care about the well-being of others as well as their own. Now the thoroughgoing egoist living by an autonomous life-plan will certainly face conflicts among preferences. But he will not face *moral* conflicts, because morality is not a category which exists for him, at least in the conduct of his own life. If he is almost late for an important appointment and on the way to it he is stopped by a foreign visitor who is thoroughly lost and needs help, he will not see the situation as involving a conflict of interests which needs to be resolved impartially, i.e. without prejudice in favour of either party. He *may* see a different conflict here, but it could only be a conflict between means to ends: will he benefit more by ignoring the visitor, even though he has built himself up a reputation for helpfulness and someone may well be present at the scene and reveal his hypocrisy; or will he do better to keep up moral appearances?

The morally good man faces moral conflicts like this, between attending to his own concerns and attending to others', which the egoist does not. Conflicts of this kind are not isolated incidents in his life but are constantly recurring. If he is to remain an integrated person, he must have some general policy for coping with them. What kind of policy could this be?

Let us assume that he is a man living according to an autonomous life-plan which is concerned with his own well-being. He possesses, therefore, an integrated system of hierarchically organised preferences which allows him to cope, more or less, with conflicts arising between these. Now one thing he could do when faced with a moral conflict of the self versus others variety would be to try to cope with the conflict *taking this life-plan as read.* In other words, he sees it as involving a clash between two (or more) different life-plans, his own and the other person's (or persons'). There is no question of his adjusting or altering his life-plan, only a question of what weight he is to give to *his* life-plan on particular occasions as compared to others'. Given that he is to remain a fully integrated person, i.e. one who seeks to resolve perennial conflicts *of all kinds*, he will have some kind of general policy for resolving this kind of moral conflict. But, if so, how can he keep his original life-plan intact? Will he not have to *enlarge* it, so that it integrates not only conflicts between personal preferences, but also moral conflicts? And if he does enlarge it, will this not mean that he has now an enlarged conception of his own well-being, as something involving integration of both these sorts? *Ex hypothesi*, however, we are trying to imagine a person who is reluctant to expand things in this way: he sees his own well-being as something self-contained, not including moral demands within it, but, on the contrary, often opposed to them; for him his life is divided into two parts, one concerned with his own well-being and the other concerned with his moral responsibilities. How, then, can such a person both hold this compartmentalised view of his life *and* seek to integrate the conflicts which arise between the two parts? How might he go about it?

It is hard to see that any policy could be wholly successful. This is a logical point. He wants to integrate the two halves of his life, but there is no system, overarching both halves, in which he can do it. In practice, though – and bearing in mind that he might not see the logical point – there are various things he could try to do. It would be helpful to him, for instance, if the moral demands made on him were as few as possible. This would not help to resolve those moral conflicts which did arise, but it would at least reduce them to a minimum, thus preventing them from being too much of a threat to his psychic unity.

There are two ways in which moral demands could be so minimised: either the content of his morality or the occasions on which moral conflicts arose could be severely restricted. If he minimises the content of morality, he becomes the minimal moralist already discussed. As we saw earlier, it is the obligation of benevolence which the minimal moralist is most likely to play down: it is here that conflicts between one's own and others' interests are particularly liable to break out, not least if benevolence is something which one ought to show not only to a limited circle of acquaintances but to those outside this. If one's moral code is restricted to such things as rules of non-injury, truth-telling, keeping contracts and promises, respect for property etc., then conflict with one's own interests may be fairly easily avoidable: one may have acquired general dispositions to keep these rules and found that they do not often get in the way of one's pursuing one's own interests. Where they do, one can adopt as a general rule that moral obligations come first. This certainly damages one's life-plan, but for the most part it only dents it, not destroys it. *More or less* one can succeed in this way in keeping the two halves of one's life in separate compartments.

The other way of doing this is by minimising the occasions which give rise to moral conflict. One might believe, for instance, that one ought to treat the interests of those with whom one comes into face-to-face contact as generously as one treats one's own, while at the same time so arranging one's life that one comes into as little contact with others as possible. One might thus try to preserve one's psychic unity by becoming a recluse, or by living a full but self-contained life on one's own country estate, taking care to see one's servants as little as possible.

In these various ways one may try to integrate one's moral responsibilities with one's own well-being. But the resolution will not succeed. A main stumbling-block is benevolence. If there is no good reason to restrict this obligation so that it applies only to face-to-face acquaintances or any other limited circle, then one can only achieve the appearance of resolution at the cost of ignoring an essential feature of a rational morality. The man on his country estate, for instance, still has obligations of benevolence towards those whom he never meets. He can only achieve his resolution by adopting an *arbitrary* conception of morality: he can give no good reason for adopting the moral code he has. As we saw in our earlier discussion of moral minimalism, if his code is not a rationalisation of an underlying egoism, it is something which he can only follow in an unreflecting, rule-bound way, for once he began to reflect he would be in danger of seeing its irrationality.

This brings me to another way in which moral conflicts between one's own and others' interests may be prevented from affecting one's psychic unity. Let us suppose that the agent has a more generous view benevolence than the man on the country estate, not restricting it to face-to-face acquaintances. Suppose, further, that he feels that he ought not to live the sybaritic life he does, but should do much more than he does to help the really needy. Here is a genuine moral conflict between his own personal projects and his altruistic obligations. He feels guilty that he does not do what he thinks is morally right. Since Freud, especially, we are very familiar with another way of trying to minimise moral conflict – repression. The man may intentionally try to forget his guilt. He may try to put it out of his mind by various kinds of defence mechanisms. Well-heeled and on the whole humane white South Africans often seem to me to have recourse to this solution. They rationalise: the Bantu does not need white wealth because he is happy as he is or too stupid to know what to do with it. They become obsessive about things, redirecting their thoughts away from their moral problem on to buying masses of unwanted goods, for instance. They attach themselves to religious leaders who reassure them they are leading a pure and wholesome life. And so on.

This last 'solution' produces at best a superficial psychic harmony masking a deeper disunity. In this it mirrors the former 'solution', i.e. restricting the scope of morality: this, too, achieved what looked like a resolution but only at the cost of a new conflict breaking out with the demands of rationality once the arbitrariness of the restriction became clear.

As has already been said, *no* solution of the problem is possible for logical reasons. Conflicts between the two spheres cannot be resolved within any larger integrating system since *ex hypothesi* there is no such system.

If we assume that in setting forth our educational aims we are requiring at least that the pupil grows up without major psychical disunity, there seems to be only one alternative. He cannot try to keep his life-plan intact, that is, concerned only with his own well-being (or the well-being of himself and his family etc.) and hived off from wider moral considerations. His life-plan must be enlarged so as to encompass the integration of conflicts of all kinds, not only conflicts of preference but also moral conflicts. That is to say, he now has an enlarged conception of his own well-being. This consists in leading a life of moral virtue, in which his own needs and interests are not automatically given preferential treatment but are weighed in the balance with the needs of others.

There is a logical difficulty here, since it looks as if we are saying that the man's well-being consists in balancing his own well-being against others'. But we can get round this easily enough once we remember that we are using 'well-being' in the first case in its enlarged sense and in the second in its pre-enlarged sense. In its pre-enlarged sense, it is true, a man's well-being *might* consist in leading a morally virtuous life. This would depend on whether or not he happened to want to do so. But, equally, it might well *not* consist in that if the pattern of his preferences were different. The crucial feature of the enlarged sense is that it is now written into it by definition that one's master-desire is to lead a morally good life.

The way is now clear for an answer to the question that has occupied us in this section: how ought pupil-centred and moral aims of education to be related? The answer is that these two aims *do* coincide, but only if in saying that education should aim at the pupil's autonomously pursuing his own well-being, we understand 'well-being' in the enlarged sense. Given this, there need be no dispute between those who say that the main aim of education should be 'personal autonomy', 'self-realisation' or 'happiness', and those who see it as 'moral goodness', or 'the good of society'. There are all sorts of ways in which the aims associated with these terms can be taken in senses different from each other, but provided that we interpret them along the lines of the recent discussion, they can also be shown to be identical.

But this neat solution to our central problem does not take us all the way. Some would say it does not take us very far at all. For we still want to know more about the 'life of moral virtue' which the proposed master-aim involves, especially about the weight the pupil should attach to his own concerns *vis-à-vis* those of others. Bearing in mind, too, our discussion of universal morality, we need also to know more about who these 'others' are. We may also wonder about the justifiability of making the moral aim of education a *master*-aim. Is it so clear that moral considerations should override all others? And if it is not, is there not a danger of arbitrarily imposing one sort of aim at the expense of others?

These questions, as we shall see, are interconnected.

What is meant by the 'morally virtuous life' in this context? It is not the life of thoroughgoing altruism in which the agent promotes *only* others' well-being and *never* his own. The suggestion that we should all be thoroughgoing altruists is absurd. There would be no guarantee that any particular individual's needs would be attended to, since he along with everybody else might be directing his benevolence elsewhere. So some people might not be cared for at all. Thoroughgoing altruism is irrational because it does not show *why* the agent should not devote some of his attention to himself. That there is reason enough for this should be evident from what has just been said: if everyone attends to his own needs to some extent, then we will never be in the unhappy situation where some people languish simply because no one happens to be caring for them. Thoroughgoing altruism also conflicts with what we know of human nature. Every man has a natural affection for himself; and although some moralists overemphasise the self-centredness, making people incapable of any genuinely altruistic attitudes at all, they are right at least to the extent that some self-centredness is probably ineradicable. And why should we want it otherwise? What, after all, is wrong with a moderate degree of self-love? Christianity has been directly or indirectly influential in making some people feel that even the slightest self-concern is sinful. Youngsters brought up today in schools and colleges strongly imbued with a Christian ethos not infrequently hold this belief. But it is not a rational one and the sooner they give it up the better both for them and for the rest of us.

Self-concern embraces both the satisfaction of one's basic needs, or means-to-ends, and the pursuit of ends-in-themselves. In theory there is no *necessity* for the agent to bother about his own health, shelter, clothing, food etc. Others could look after all these things for him, even to the extent of dressing him or brushing his teeth. But there are obvious practical reasons why he should do much of this himself. I do not mean to draw any hard-and-fast lines in all this about what the individual should have to bother about: whether, for instance, there should be a national health service or a guaranteed minimum income for all raises large questions which we cannot go into here.

Self-concern about basic needs need not imply anything about the weighting one gives to others' well-being as against one's own : my basic needs must be satisfied whether I live a self-contained life devoted to piano-playing or spend my time working for the borough council.

So there are good enough reasons why the pupil should attend to his basic needs. They do not justify him – although other reasons might – in going beyond *minimal* requirements, in trying to get more money than he needs, for instance, or in buying a six-bedroomed house when a three-bedroomed one will do. Again, no hard-and-fast lines can be drawn to demarcate minima.

What about his ends-in-themselves? To be sure, his master-end will be the life of moral virtue itself, but falling under that will be other ends which are more self-referential. These range from those which are *purely* self-regarding such as playing the piano for enjoyment without ever performing in front of others, to those touching the well-being of others closely connected with oneself, like enjoying a family holiday. What weight should the pupil put on self-referring ends like these as against more altruistic ends?

Different moralities, as we have seen, embody different emphases. Minimalist morality stresses his own ends, universalism, everyone's. We have already seen the difficulties with both extremes. The least we can do by the pupil is to make him as aware as possible of these difficulties and of the ineradicable tensions there must be between the two poles. We can then leave it to him, as a morally autonomous agent, to strike his own balances.

This is certainly preferable to bringing him up firmly within one or other of the opposing moralities. That would be to shut him off both from its problems and from the virtues of its competitors. It would be to indoctrinate him in a particular set of beliefs and attitudes.

But what would it be to bring him up in the open-minded way recommended? It would not be to let him think he can weight things how he wants according only to personal preference. This would be not to take seriously his enmeshment in a *moral* conflict. There are reasons favouring his attending impartially to everybody's interests and there are reasons why attempting consistently to do this leads to absurdity. In favouring one set of interests over another he will be aware of the serious reasons which might have inclined him to strike the balance in another place.

Is there any more specific advice that educators would be justified in giving him, or must they simply leave him to struggle along on his own? One thing they could remind him of is the absurdity of thoroughgoing altruism, along with its important corollary that, given the point of morality is the promotion of people's well-being, and given that each of us has an inalienable interest in his own well-being, moral aims may often best be served by leaving each individual plenty of space to pursue his own ends. Another relevant consideration is the particular nature of the world in which he lives and of his position in it. A century ago T. H. Green, affected by the inhuman conditions in which many were living at that time, wrote:

> It is no time to enjoy the pleasures of eye and ear, of search for knowledge, of friendly intercourse, of applauded speech or writing, while the mass of men whom we call our brethren ... are left without the chance, which only the help of others can gain for them, of making themselves in act what in possibility we believe them to be (Green, 1883, p. 270).

In a society where everyone was plentifully supplied with the necessities of life, it would be irrational to be moved by the thought of what one might do to help the suffering masses, since no one would be suffering. The more people got on with their aesthetic and other pleasures the better. The question the pupil should ask himself is: what kind of a society do I live in? Is my own country sufficiently affluent and well-educated that there is little call for benevolence on a mass scale? If so, does this mean that more of us are justified in spending more time on our own concerns? Or does it mean that we should spend more time on helping distress elsewhere in the world? To what extent does Green's plea now become relevant at the international, rather than at the national, level?

As well as the state of his society and of the world, the pupil also needs to take account of his own position in society. He will occupy various sorts of role within that society, including, as is likely, occupational roles. How is he to see the job he will be doing? Many jobs obviously help other people: growing food, teaching children to read, digging drains and so on. Others – advertising, perhaps, or working on tabloid dailies – are more indeterminate in their benefits, if any. Most jobs, in addition, can be done partly or wholly for self-interested reasons, because pay and conditions are good, for instance, or because they are the lesser of two evils. In weighing out what portion of his life he will spend in the service of others, it will be important to him to reflect on the type of work he might choose to do from the point of view of its benefits to others and to himself.

There is another way in which the pupil should take account of his own social position. Suppose he ends up with a tedious, dead-end job which means that he has to live in poverty – if not in material poverty then in the spiritual poverty which can come from spending half one's waking hours doing a mechanical job and the other half recovering from it. Or suppose he ends up in some other way severely disadvantaged: perhaps he does not even have a job at all. From a moral point of view he deserves others' help. But since he, too, is looking at his own social position impartially, from the same point of view, he has good reason to lay particular weight on his own interests. Poorly off workers in our society are often accused of 'selfishness' if they strike for better wages or conditions. But they have absolutely no reason to feel guilty about putting themselves first. On the contrary, they are doing what is morally right.

While the disadvantaged are morally justified in tilting the scales away from altruism, so those who find themselves well off must beware lest they tilt them too far towards their own interests. This is especially true in a society where moral minimalism is particularly strong among the better-off.

There are other reminders, too, which may be useful to him. About the ways, for instance, in which one's own well-being may be entwined with that of others. Men who live only for their own self-fulfilment through art can provide enjoyment and insight for millions. So a 'self-centred' way of life may turn out to be not so self-centred after all. Of course, a person who follows this path, realising its moral potentialities, would do best to make sure that he has the necessary talents to bring the altruistic benefits.

One of the consequences of opening the pupil's eyes as widely as possible to all the manifold ways of life from which he can choose – an educational aim which I have argued for in this book – is that it is likely to lead to a sense of regret that he cannot do everything that he would like to. Life is short. One cannot be a professional musician and an airline pilot and a lawyer; one cannot be a Muslim and a Christian and an atheist, a recluse and a social reformer. For this very reason one may welcome and encourage the existence of other people who *do* lead these other ways of life towards which one is attracted. Identifying with other people may help one, as it were, to make one's life more complete, less full of unrealised possibilities. Helping others achieve their goals may, therefore, at the same time help one to realise one's own.

Finally, as Butler pointed out, the benevolent man is in one way more certain to achieve his own well-being than the egoist, who aims directly at achieving it (Butler, 1726, Sermon 11). The latter may fail: the benefits he intends to procure himself may be frustrated, for instance, by events beyond his control. The benevolent man may fail in the same way: his Oxfam money may be embezzled on its way to India. But he does succeed in acting with a benevolent *intention* whatever the outcome of the action. He is on a winning horse in the desire-satisfaction stakes.

I do not mean to imply in any of these last two cases that one should act benevolently for the sake of one's own well-being. This would be to make what seemed to be morally virtuous behaviour into something merely prudential. The only point I am making, as in the first case, is about the way which one's own and others' well-being are often closely interconnected: it may be illuminating to the pupil to be aware of this.

Chapter 5

The good of society (2): moral aims in their economic and political aspects

The last two chapters have stated the main theses about educational aims discussed in this book. This chapter extends the argument in favour of moral autonomy into two related areas, the economic and the political. The first extension takes us back into the topic of 'education for work' which we broached at the beginning of chapter 4. The second discusses 'citizenship' as an aim of education.

Moral aims and economic aims

How are the moral and economic aims of education to be related?

'Moral training' has always been a high priority among those wanting to orient education towards industry and commerce. Employers want workers who are honest, punctual, industrious, co-operative and above all obedient. They want them by and large to do what their foremen and managers tell them and without any fuss. But 'being morally virtuous' in this sense is a far cry from the similarly named educational ideal of the last section. Morally autonomous people cannot be unquestioningly obedient.

Obedience is, in any case, not a moral virtue. Neither are employers and industrially oriented educationists, for all their emphasis on 'moral training', much interested in morality at all. What they really want is employees who do what they are told. What the workers' reasons may be for complying is of less importance. It does not matter if they toe the line for purely prudential reasons, to avoid dismissal, for instance, or in the hope of promotion.

Prudential reasons for action are widespread, in fact, in modern industry. R. H. Tawney drew our attention long ago to early capitalism's attempts to hive off economic activity from the moral sphere (Tawney, 1926). The same compartmentalism is still powerful today. It lies behind moral minimalism. In industrial terms it takes the form of wanting market forces to determine each aspect of the industrial process, unfettered as far as possible by moral considerations. Employees contract to sell their labour for a wage. They are attracted into and held in jobs by hope of reward and fear of punishment. What is produced is what is profitable: newspaper companies do not typically scrutinise their products for their moral acceptability and decide not to produce them if they don't do people any good. If it is profitable to extend the market for their goods, companies invest in advertising campaigns but do not typically reflect on the rightness or wrongness of trying to create new wants in people by non-rational forms of persuasion.

Government action has helped to bring economic activity under moral constraints to a large extent: firms are bound by regulations of all sorts, to do with industrial safety, the sale and advertising of harmful products, the description of goods and so on. But although *legislators* have been morally motivated in this way, this says nothing about the attitudes of those working in industry. Companies can and do still try to operate for largely prudential reasons within these 'external' constraints.

The ideal of moral autonomy clashes head-on with prevailing attitudes in industry. Imagine a pupil educated on the lines proposed in the last chapter taking his first job on the shop-floor of a factory producing white sliced bread. He is told to do such and such an operation, expected to get on with it quietly and ask no questions. But as a morally autonomous person how can he *not* ask questions? Questions of all sorts. What kind of product is it? Does it do people any good? (I choose white sliced bread since there is an increasing amount of evidence to show that much factory-made bread is physically harmful.) Is it right to advertise it extensively so as to get people to buy it? Is the company out primarily to give a service or to make a profit? Is it right that profit goes to shareholders, or should more of it go to the employees, or to the government? Is it right that the company should be hierarchically arranged, with those at higher levels telling those at lower levels what to do? Is it right that there should be such disparities of income for those at different levels of the hierarchy? And so on.

I am aware that many employers would shudder at the thought of the education system's deliberately setting out to produce pupils disposed to subject their work to moral scrutiny in this way. 'Things are bad enough as they are', one can almost hear them complaining. 'Today's work-force is bolshie enough as it is, without the schools goading it still further.' I suspect, too, that if this book ever gets noticed it will be branded in some quarters as a radically leftist tract which seeks to undermine the whole basis of our economy and indoctrinate new generations of schoolchildren in the ideology of revolution. I cannot help what people might call it. The reasons for insisting on moral autonomy as an educational aim have already been spelt out. Here I am merely looking at some of the consequences of taking this aim seriously. The morally autonomous man cannot obediently knuckle under. He is morally obliged to ask these questions. If, as a result of this happening on a large enough scale, present-day capitalism fails to survive its 'legitimation crisis' and is transformed into something more acceptable, that will be all to the good (cf. Habermas, 1976).

Moral autonomy among employees threatens not only employers but also trades unions. Here, too, there are hierarchies, demands to toe the line, self-protective policies which may not always be morally defensible. The same moral probing is only to be expected here as well.

All this points to the need for new forms of work-place democracy to institutionalise moral autonomy among employees. For it is not enough for them to be able to ask awkward questions in a detached way. As moral agents, their main concern is not just to think, but to act. If companies are run democratically so that each employee can have some hand in running his firm, no one need feel that decisions about his work are being made for him, over which he has no control (see P. White, 1979).

What form this democratic organisation should take is a further question beyond our immediate concerns. So, too, are details about income distribution, the human value of what is produced etc. In setting out educational aims we can only point in general directions. But one thing our present discussion shows – and this is a point taken up again in chapter 7 – is that it is not only homes, schools and colleges which can have a hand in realising the aims of education. The way other, e.g. industrial, institutions are organised can also help or hinder their achievement. As things are now, they are often an impediment to moral autonomy. But they could be reorganised along democratic lines to maintain and deepen attitudes already formed at school.

What is being proposed, therefore, is a subjugation of economic to moral aims and not vice versa. This applies not only to the time when pupils are already at work but also to when they are choosing what job to do. In constructing their enlarged, i.e. moralised, life-plan, pupils need to weigh the altruistic as well as the self-centred benefits likely to accrue from jobs of different sorts in their moral balance. It should not be enough for them to look at costs and benefits in an amoralised way.

This is a convenient point at which explicitly to interrelate all *three* aims we have been looking at in this and in previous chapters – moral, economic and pupil-centred. I argued at the beginning of chapter 4 that economic aims must be subordinated to the kind of pupil-centred aim favoured in chapter 3. Since then I have suggested that this pupil-centred aim should be expanded so that pupils see their own well-being as consisting in a life of moral virtue. Economic aims, we have now seen, are also to be subjugated to pupil-centred aims in the enlarged sense.

I perhaps need to make it quite clear in this connection – if it is not abundantly clear already – that in pressing for morally autonomous employees I am not thinking of a work-force of thoroughgoing altruists, self-sacrificingly getting their companies on an even moral keel. The morally autonomous man is not a complete altruist, for reasons already given. As a worker, as a participant in his work-place democracy, he will weigh his own claims in the balance along with other people's. If he is relatively disadvantaged, as I pointed out in an earlier section, he is *morally* fully entitled to stand up for himself and press for better wages and conditions of work. In doing so he is not acting selfishly in despite of his moral obligations: he is carrying out those obligations up to the hilt.

Citizenship as an aim

Citizenship has always been included in the lists of educational aims, either as a master-aim embracing all others or as one aim among many. How does it fit into the structure of aims built up in the last two chapters?

Let me first clear out of the way senses in which I am not using the term. Totalitarian states usually highlight this aim, but more often than not as a euphemism for blind obedience to a ruling elite. Sometimes, too, the term can apply, in totalitarian and non-totalitarian states alike, to both elite and masses, meaning not the kind of obedience just mentioned, but a chauvinistic attachment to one's country or nation. As an over-arching aim of education this must be rejected, for it fails the test of impartiality and arbitrarily puts the interests of one country above all others.

In what more justifiable sense, then, can one advocate education for citizenship? The section on concrete morality showed how in the idealist tradition the state-community has mediated between the individual and mankind as a whole, making concrete the former's moral obligations to the latter. We have already pointed to the deficiencies of seeing all one's wider moral concerns as *having* to be mediated *via* the state: one can go off to work among the poor in the Third World as a nun or in a relief agency. But, even so, the state *can* be a mediator and one should not overlook its potential moral role internationally. Besides this, we do need to live our moral lives in a concrete way: when we think about our obligations to others, we do have to work with some fairly determinate picture of who these 'others' might be. The state-community provides one forum − not necessarily the most important − in which our moral aspirations can be realised. As our recent discussion of the moral organisation of industry shows, many of the moral issues which present themselves to the autonomous worker cannot be solved within the company, but only at a higher level. The state is one such level − and not only for industrial matters, but also for policies on welfare services, law and order, education and many other things.

But why turn to the *state* as a moral framework? Why not a smaller-scale community − an anarchist commune, kibbutz or other variant? Apart from the obvious danger of communal egoism − of living only for itself and ignoring the needs of those outside it − a small community might limit the individual's picture of the world and of human life. If the community is very small, this is all but unavoidable. Assuming that it does not rest on a basis of slavery, much of its time will be taken up with agriculture, simple manufactures, etc. It will not have much time for reflection about larger matters. Neither will it contain many people who could engage in this reflection. So its ideological basis is likely to be a narrow one, comprising few if any alternative perspectives. It does not follow, of course, that the larger a community is, the more catholic its ideology will be: it could still be a totalitarian community of a religious or other kind. But at least in a larger community there is the *opportunity*, provided that steps are taken to prevent totalitarianism, to encourage a breadth of views about the conduct of life.

It is hard to see how the well-being of small-scale communities could be the sole object of educational endeavour. This is not to say that small communities are wholly unimportant: they can play a vital part within larger wholes. But on their own they are probably unable to realise the well-being, as we have defined it, of all their members. We now reach something like the point which Hegel reached in rejecting the Greek city-state or *polis*, despite its strong sense of community, as an ideal. What the *polis* lacked, in Hegel's view, was a belief in that freedom of the individual – every individual – which the Enlightenment saw as important for the fully rational life and the highest flights of human expressiveness. Hegel's own preferred alternative was the Hegelian state, which married the Greek ideal of community to the Enlightenment ideal of freedom.

Can we go so far, without commitment to Hegel, as to assert that one aim of education should be that the pupil should promote the well-being of the state?

If we do, the fears of those who think that emphasising the social aims of education might soon lead us towards totalitarianism might seem well-founded. But let us try to put our emotive reactions to the phrase 'education for the state' on one side, if we can. Part of the reason for our alarm is the thought that education for the state is really education for the State, with a capital S: children will have to be so educated that their lives are dedicated to the service of a supra-personal entity which does not exist. In fact this will mean sacrificing them to the interests of whatever power-group can trick the people into believing that the State exists and that they are its trustees.

But 'state' need not be written with a capital S. One common way of understanding a 'state' today is as a government machine. The state is not to be identified with the government of the day, since it persists in its identity through changes of government. It is rather, the machine that the government oversees, including in our case the Civil Service in its different departments, the Bank of England and other nationalised enterprises. Taken like this, the state hardly seems to be a proper object of educational concern in its own right. It would be very odd to claim that education should aim at promoting the well-being of the Civil Service or the National Coal Board.

But in this section we have already been working with a *third* conception of a state – a state as a form of community. Like other communities, the family, for instance, it consists of individuals in relationship to each other; its well-being is that of these related individuals. Individuals are related together within the family directly, within the state indirectly, via their membership of other intermediate institutions – families, work-groups etc. In the state-community the work and lives of these institutions and individuals are harmonised so that they co-operate – to some extent – for common ends. This harmonising can be achieved by the laws and regulations which the governing organs of the state enforce and sometimes bring into being; and it can also be achieved by other forms of persuasion. In advanced industrial states, the government machine can become very large and complex – so complex that one can easily come to identify this machine with the state itself. What makes it tempting to do so is that the way in which states differ from smaller communities is in being regulated by a government machine. But necessarily possessing a government machine is not to be confused with necessarily *being* such a machine.

Some will object to this third conception of the state on the grounds that a 'state-community' is no community at all, as it is too large. Communities are joined together by fraternal bonds, born of co-operation for shared ends. These can exist in small groups but not, so it is often argued, in large ones numbering several millions. At least, not normally. When Hitler reached Dunkirk, there *did* spring into being a common purpose which helped to unite the British into a fraternal community. But the fraternity did not survive the war. J. D. Mabbott argues in this way in *The State and the Citizen* (p. 95), attacking the notion of the service of the state as the moral ideal. But his is a very black-and-white view. Fraternity is a matter of degree. It may be strongest in a small group but need not be entirely absent in a large. If we remember that the state-community is not an amorphous heap of individuals but includes smaller mediating groups of all kinds, there is no reason why the currents of co-operativeness and fellow-feeling which run through the latter should not circulate, albeit less swiftly, through the body politic as a whole.

Education for citizenship could be seen, in short, as education for membership of a state-community of this kind. The latter could obviously still be interpreted in different ways. One example would be Hegel's state. There are problems about this – not least the assumption that it mediates between man and God (or Spirit) – but we shall not pursue them here. A second interpretation would be of a state-community characterised by the autonomy, including the moral autonomy, described earlier in this book. Given this, the claim that one aim of education should be that the pupil come to see himself as a member of a state, co-operating fraternally for shared ends, may become more attractive than when the only senses we could attach to 'state' were those of a supra-personal entity, a government machine, or a monolithic community.

Even so, we have to tread carefully. The idealist picture of the state-community as the chief forum for our moral life can be too seductive, especially if one writes into it that the state is not exclusivist towards those outside it. It can be very tempting to think of the education as nothing more than preparation for citizenship within such a state-community, since all attachments to smaller groups can be represented as attachments to the state in one or other of its articulations. The problem with this is that there seems no good reason why *one* framework within which our moral lives can be led should be picked out as *the* framework *par excellence*. We are moral agents on a number of different levels, ranging from self- or domestic concerns through to obligations towards mankind as a whole. One of these levels is the level of the state-community. But there is no reason to elevate this over all others. It is certainly aesthetically attractive to reconceptualise all one's smaller-scale moral attachments (e.g. to one's family) and all one's larger-scale moral attachments (e.g. to mankind) as aspects of one's citizenship within the state. But moral reality is messier. The idealist view would leave no room for one's helping those outside one's state-community except as an agent of that community. It would have to exclude institutions, e.g. industrial companies or artistic societies, which had some kind of world-wide organisation but none at the level of the state. Not all our moral life must be mediated by the state. In addition the idealist view stresses moral harmony too much at the expense of moral conflict. My interest in myself or my family can conflict with my role as worker, citizen, or member of the world community. There is no common good which can show me that these conflicts are after all illusory: they are real, and only I can integrate them. It is very important not to go all the way down the idealist road, because it ends up, once again, and despite its good intentions, only in imposing an unjustified picture of the moral life on the pupil. He is not to be indoctrinated into the view that only in his civic life can he achieve full moral self-realisation.

At the same time – and this is the positive point we can extract from the doctrine – it is equally vital to reveal to him the opportunities which membership of a state-community affords him and the obligation it lays on him to enlarge his moral horizons. Our recoil from the once popular idea of 'education for the state', fully understandable though it is in the light of twentieth-century experience, has gone too far.

I have been careful in this section not to equate state with nation. A nation could be divided into two or more states: the German nation today, for instance (overlooking the fact that both West and East

Germany are in different ways very imperfect specimens of the state-ideal I have outlined). Great Britain could in principle break up – and some might think it should – into eight or ten small-size state-communities. On the other hand, a state-community *could* be co-extensive with a nation. It is an interesting question whether or not there would be any dangers or difficulties if it were.

Let us approach this from the side of education. If the state-community were a nation, education for a state-community would become education for the nation; children would be brought up, in our country, as patriotic members of the British nation; education would be shot through with nationalism: 'And it is obvious where this would end', many will say. 'Surely, after the world wars this century has seen, the *last* thing we want is a nationalistic education.'

Once again, though, we should not allow ourselves to be carried away by the emotive power of words. T. H. Green spoke of the modern state as in most cases 'an organisation of a people to whom the individual feels himself bound by ties analogous to those which bind him to his family, ties derived from a common dwelling-place with its associations, from common memories, traditions and customs, and from common ways of feeling and thinking which a common language and still more a common literature embodies' (Green, 1883, para. 123). The individual's attachment to humanity as a whole needs, as we have seen, to be localised in smaller-scale community life. A group speaking a common language is an obvious candidate for this role. If features like this are not present, then other things must be found as a focus. Sometimes they can be: at other times and in other places – in continental Europe, for instance – it might not be easy to do so.

It would be foolish, then, to overlook the possibilities which national characteristics can provide of helping to bind together a state-community. To say this is not to embrace the *exclusiveness* of nationalism – the feeling that one's own nation is better than, greater than, more important than others. There is nothing to be said for this communal selfishness. But there are enough examples in the world today of nation-states whose basic ideology is universalistic rather than exclusive to show that national feeling, or patriotism, in this deliberately watered-down sense, is not at all incompatible with the idea of an outward-looking state-community as outlined in this book.

Whether it is best for state-communities to be based on national characteristics is a question to which there is no general answer. Perhaps new foci of community could and should be found. Perhaps there is something in the arguments of those who say that large societies tend towards alienation and that communities should be on a smaller scale. As I have said, to some extent this argument can be met by pointing out the role which intermediate communities can play in binding the individual to the larger state-community. But the comeback to this might be that although this solution is always *possible*, it is not *practicable* given the nature of the work- and other institutions we have today and the unlikelihood of the state-community's being able to harmonise their operations without turning society into a giant bureaucratic machine. No one, I think, is in any authoritative position to say whether territorial states as we know them today can, or cannot, be transformed into something more ideal. If so, then children should be deliberately educated as citizens in such a way as to leave this question unresolved. In their generation, with new technological inventions, perhaps, and with more experience of the conditions in which societies remain in harmony or fall apart, they may well be in a better position to answer it than we can now.

What can we say about the internal arrangement of the state-community, regardless of its size? How is it to be politically organised? Will it be in any sense a class society?

Contemporary British society is still influenced to a remarkable degree by a nineteenth-century conception of education which is clearly Platonic: while the great mass of the population are thought to need an education which fits them for certain kinds of jobs, and gives them no deeper understanding of society as a whole than these particular roles require, those who will belong to a ruling elite are held to need a more rounded education. The ideal is of a 'liberal' education for these few and a 'vocational' education for the rest. For some, the line between the two is to be drawn between the independent and the maintained school sectors. On one side of this line, the ideal picture is of public schools providing a rich, many-sided education as a basis for a university education which, though often more specialised in its formal curriculum than work at school, helps to initiate the future members of the elite into a wider social understanding and strengthen the fraternal links between them by all sorts of extra-curricular activities. Below the line, we have a maintained sector, preferably, though not necessarily, divided between schools for Auxiliaries of the elite and schools for the rest. Neither of these types of school is to provide a synoptic education. Grammar schools, or the GCE streams of comprehensive schools, should produce the knowledgeable technicians, managers and other experts which an advanced economy needs; while secondary-modern schools or the non-GCE streams in comprehensives should produce school leavers who have attained minimum, and generally no more than minimum standards, in 'core' areas like literacy and arithmetic as well as having, in many cases, some of the specialised skills needed in the lower ranks of industry.

Leaving the details of our British experience on one side, we have here an educational ideal which can be realised in a wide variety of different contexts. Its central feature is that only the elite which has to do with the spiritual-political functions of the community – its artists, thinkers, statesmen, judges, higher civil servants etc. – will need a synoptic education which will take them into the heart of problems of human well-being, while others – farmers, engineers, machine operators and so on – do not need this understanding and commitment in order to perform their specialised functions. Politics need not concern them. They could, indeed, be guided by a conventional, non-autonomous morality, doing their work well, for instance, because it is expected of them, and not because they understand its contribution to the social whole. Unlike the rulers, it does not matter if they are left in ignorance of everything except their special skill or trade. It may not help the well-being of the state if they are more autonomous or more knowledgeable. On the contrary, if the mass of the people *did* begin to work for common ends as they saw them, there would be a danger of disco-ordination between the different social functions which they performed, for their understanding of what was in the common interest might well differ among themselves. Better, then, to leave social policy to those trained to deal with it: social order is likely to be better achieved by encouraging the masses to live for themselves and their families and leave a wider morality to others. Similarly with the extent of their knowledge: if they know only what is necessary for their particular job, it can be left to the rulers, with their broader knowledge, to co-ordinate the work of those below them. The more the latter know outside their job, however, the greater the danger, once again, that they will meddle with wider matters of statecraft and produce more disruption of the social order.

Accepting *pro tem.* the implied importance of social cohesion, is it true that the 'Platonic' society is more likely to promote it than any other? The Platonic position seems to rest on the claim that it is in principle possible to train up a class of men to be authorities on the ends which the state-community should follow.

If there were such infallible procedures, it might well be better to leave the determination of final ends to a ruling class. But despite Plato's conviction that moral experts exist, ethical theory since his time has failed to reveal them. It may or may not be true that there can be expertise of a kind when it comes to reflecting on the nature of morality; but even if moral philosophers could see more clearly than others the basic principles on which any morality must rest (and this may be in doubt), philosophers have no special insight into how principles are to be applied in particular cases. So philosophers cannot be relied on to determine the political ends of a society. Economists and other social scientists may be in a better position than others to work out the likely consequences of following policy A rather than policy B. But they have no special authority, which the rest of the population lacks, to say that we *should* follow A rather than B. No one is in a privileged position to say what our communal ends shall be. If so, the rationale for a separate ruling class, and hence a separate education, seems to have disappeared.

There seems no justification, therefore, for restricting the content of anyone's education. All, not some, should receive a synoptic rather than a narrowly specialised education. This is true, too, for another reason. If only some are to receive a synoptic education, the fraternal attitudes necessary to the well-being of the state-community will be put at risk. Let us call the group to which the synoptic education has been confined 'A' and the rest of the population 'B'. Now members of A, we may imagine, are bound tightly together by fraternal ties: they see themselves each as self-consciously co-operating with others among them for common ends. They also feel something in common with members of B: they, too, are fellow-members of the same community, contributing to its well-being, albeit in their case without the larger awareness of the role they are playing. But what of members of B? What can they feel towards members of A? They cannot see them as co-workers for the same end since they lack the intellectual equipment necessary to understand this. They cannot see the point of intellectual enquiries: those who engage in such pursuits must be utterly alien figures, seen perhaps as involved in something awesome and mysterious, or perhaps more cynically, as living off the sweat of working men and idling away their lives in useless pastimes. Rulers and teachers must be similarly alien. Fraternity in this kind of society is mutual only within A; between A and B it is unidirectional, from A to B, but not vice versa – and even here members of A can only feel a *modified* form of fraternity towards members of B, since they can see them only as partially like themselves, and that not in the most important matters. This kind of society lacks the full mutuality of fraternal feeling which a community proper must possess. Only A is really a community: at best its members are deceiving themselves when they see B as forming, with themselves, a larger community; at worst their expression of this latter belief is cynical rhetoric.

For all these reasons, the well-being of the community would be better served by a common system of education of what I have telegraphically called a 'synoptic' kind, than by a divided system whereby some get a synoptic but most a specialised upbringing. While this does not entail that the content of every child's education must be identical to every other's in every detail, it does set limits to permissible variations between contents.

It is implicit in this argument for a universal synoptic education that the community will be democratically governed. At the basis of a belief in democracy is the fact that no one is in an authoritative position to determine the good of the community. No member of the community is any more an authority on political ends than any other. It would be wrong, therefore, for anyone blindly to follow another's political direction under the illusion that his guide knows where he should be leading him. *Someone* must make political decisions, however. But since no one is in a privileged position to do so, it follows that everyone has an equal right to make them. Not only is there an equal *right*: if individuals have a moral duty not to do something just because someone else tells them to, but only because they believe it is right to do, then they each have an equal *obligation* to participate, as well.

Politically, therefore, the community must be so organised as to ensure maximal participation by its members. Machinery will have to be devised to respect the moral autonomy and responsibility of the citizens – an official opposition, a free press, periodic elections, safeguards for minorities etc. etc. *Maximal* participation will also mean that democratic decision-making is not restricted to central government. The argument against the possibility of moral/political experts (i.e. the argument in favour of the moral/political autonomy of all citizens) applies at every level of community life. There is no more reason for factory workers, for instance, to carry out the orders of a permanent body of managers than there is for the people as a whole to obey a permanent central oligarchy. As has already been argued, industrial, or work-place, democracy is as essential as political. Education for a democratic community is, among other things, education for work-place democracy (P. White, 1979).

Included in this education, therefore, will be a specifically political element. In one sense, the sense in which Plato or Aristotle understood it, much of the rest of education ought to be political: that is, it ought, among other things, to fit the pupil for the best possible form of life within a state–, or political, community. In a narrower sense, political material will form only one element in the total content of an education of this kind. Citizens will all have to have at least some understanding of the principles of democracy; some empirical understanding of their actual political situation at different levels of community life and of forms of knowledge (e.g. economics, political science) which bear on the political decisions they will have to make; and a ready disposition to apply all this understanding in the service of the community.

But this more narrowly political part of the citizen's education is not finally separable from his initiation into those arts and forms of thought which reveal to him different perspectives on ultimate values, since understanding why the democratic state-community is worth defending inevitably implies that one has reflected on the nature of the *summum bonum*. Not only politics, but also philosophy, art, religion, science – all these must enter into the ordinary citizen's education.

Many will see difficulties in this kind of prescription for a common education. Some will argue that it is pitched at too high a level: only a few will be capable of it. Something like a Platonic system is, on this view, inevitable after all. There may indeed not be moral or political authorities, but it does not follow from this that *everybody* should play a part in government at different levels, and hence require the synoptic education suggested. Only those intellectually capable of doing so can do so. But the intellectual requirements are so high, involving an awareness of the nature of the good, fundamental political principles, a grasp of economics, an appreciation of the role of art in human life, and so on, that these must surely be confined to a brilliant few.

It is true that my position assumes that we all have the intellectual ability to be able to participate in democratic decision-making. This is only one of a number of empirical assumptions about human nature which I make in this book. Another, perhaps less contentious, is that we all have a capacity for fraternal feelings towards each other, that we are not all irretrievably locked in our own private egocentric worlds. Am I justified in my assumption about intellectual capacity? There is first of all the question what this capacity is for. *How much* understanding of the nature of the good, of democratic principles, of economics etc. etc. am I demanding? I would answer that understanding is a matter of degree: there can be greater or less understanding of these and other matters.

The objector's case may look strong because he is assuming that only a very high degree of understanding will do – the sort we might expect from a Platonic guardian, for instance. But I see no need for stipulating this. There is no *a priori* reason to think that democracy cannot work with less; and some empirical evidence to show that it can and does.[1] (Just what kinds of knowledge are required, and by whom, are further questions to which philosophers of education among others are now giving attention.)[2]

But I am not in any case assuming that ordinary men are incapable of a very high degree of understanding. Why should they be? The onus is on the objector to show that this is so. Appeals to experience – to the fact that schoolteachers find real intellectual ability only in a few, for instance – do not take one very far. For the shortcomings of the many in the far from perfect conditions in which they are currently educated do not prove the shortcomings of the many in a less imperfect system. Appeals to 'science', i.e. to the body of doctrine built up around the IQ–test, are scarcely more impressive, as recent criticism of these researches shows. It is hard to see *what* kind of test, IQ or any other, could show that the ordinary man has an intellectual ceiling which prevents him from making progress beyond a certain point. I have discussed such ceilings-arguments already.

If a common education of the sort envisaged is to be brought into being, it must go hand in hand with other changes in our social attitudes and practices (which may be a third reason why some will find it hard to accept). Above all, it is quite incompatible with the currently widespread view that people's levels of educational attainment should vary with their occupational stratum, that the sort of education fitted for the 'professional classes' is not at all fitted for, say, manual workers like road-menders or coal-miners. If everyone were given a common education of this kind, there might be all kinds of important consequences. There might, for instance, be more competition for jobs in which one can make use of the intellectual powers which one's education has developed. Some critics will see this as an objection to a common education, on the grounds that unsuccessful competitors – perhaps the majority of the population – will have to make do with intellectually undemanding jobs in which they will feel miserable and frustrated. But such critics lack imagination: they assume too many features of the *status quo*. Increased competition for stimulating jobs could mean that conditions of work in unstimulating jobs would have to be improved, so as to attract people into them. Perhaps a road-mender, for instance, could be paid the same for three hours' work a day as a university teacher for ten, thus leaving him time for intellectual activities outside his job. No doubt, too, one's status would come to seem less important than one's function. Few in our present society are eager to become road-menders – and would be equally reluctant even if they were well-paid for only a couple of hours' work a day. Who would willingly choose to become 'the lowest of the low', a person who causes men's eyes to be turned away in embarrassment when they pass him in the road? Yet why do we not value the work of the road-mender, the sewerage-worker, the office-cleaner, the textile-mill machinist or the postman just as much as we do that of the professor or artist or statesman? In a better society than ours such 'lowly' jobs would have no stigma. People would be less fussy about what kind of job they did as long as it was important in this extended sense, and given that they had adequate opportunities to realise their spiritual capacities, either inside or outside their job. Many would, I dare say, *prefer* a humdrum job – being a milkman, say – at least for part of their lives, on the grounds that they would then be more certain of doing something beneficial to the community than if they were, say, a painter or a teacher or a politician. Milk is delivered, people are nourished; but projected masterpieces can fail to be realised, pupils may not learn, laws not get passed. Have I myself and my colleagues followed the right road in becoming university teachers rather than, say, bakery-workers? ('How unthinkable, after all their education!') To convince ourselves that we have, how much anguish and effort should we have to put into our job, so as to be less likely to look back at the end of our careers and be ashamed of how little we have achieved! Who would not rather have been a maker of a million loaves when it comes to the day of judgment?[3]

This concludes what I want to say about citizenship as an aim. Except for one thing. I have stressed that pupils should see that they have not merely the *right* to participate in democratic decision-making at different levels, but also the *duty* to do so. Many of the moral decisions in which they will be implicated, as parents, workers, citizens and in other roles, directly or indirectly, require resolution at a political level. But none of this implies that every pupil shall become a political activist. How different individuals weight their civic responsibilities as against other things may vary from one to another. How are these responsibilities to be balanced against one's desire to exploit one's unusual musical talent, or against family commitments, or against one's work for Oxfam? We are back with the old problem of incommensurable moral demands and must leave it, as always, to the autonomous moral agent to make his own judgment on the balances to be struck among them. But even if he devotes himself – on a private income – to the oboe and never votes or reads a newspaper, this would not, on the educational ideal suggested here, be as a result of mere political apathy. It would not be that he 'couldn't care less about politics'. His understanding of his citizenly role would bring him to *care* well enough. But his commitment to music would have a higher moral priority for him, so much higher, indeed, that it could leave no room for political involvement, however minimal. Actually I doubt whether anyone's honest moral reflections could lead him to establish quite so extreme an order of priorities as this, although less stark conflicts are easily imaginable. But even in so extreme a case the musician cannot lightly shrug politics aside. It is hard to see how he can avoid some kind of feeling of trepidation lest his talent, say, does not finally justify his single-mindedness or, more generally, lest his balance is not struck exactly where it ought to be. The musician's is, as I have said, an extreme case. He has made a once-for-all decision to exclude politics from his life. In actuality, of course, people rarely see it as reasonable to make such once-for-all decisions. Balancing priorities is something we typically must do and redo throughout our lives. Our civic obligations are always with us.[4]

Chapter 6

The educated man

A sketch of his achievements

We have reached the end of our survey of educational aims and must take stock. What picture of the educated man has emerged?

It has grown broader and broader in scope from our early discussion of intrinsic aims through pupil oriented and into society oriented aims. The educated man is someone who has come to care about his own well-being in the extended sense which includes his living a morally virtuous life, this latter containing a civic dimension among others. Whereas other recent accounts of him have made his possession of *knowledge* his chief characteristic, this one makes *virtues* more central. The educated man is a man disposed to act in certain ways rather than others. He possesses the general virtue of prudence, or care for his own good (as well as subordinate virtues like courage and temperance). This, being in an extended rather than a narrow sense, includes within it the more specifically moral virtues like benevolence, justice, truthfulness, tolerance and reliability. It includes both the lucidity needed to sort out clearly the complex conflicts of value which face him, and the wisdom needed to reflect on these conflicts and try to resolve them within as broad a framework of relevant considerations as possible. The educated man, prizing autonomy, will be independent-minded himself and sympathetic to independent-mindedness in others. His ability to detach himself from narrow ends and to enter imaginatively into others' points of view makes it inconceivable that he be the kind of humourless person we can all number among our so-called 'educated' acquaintances. As well as all this, one may expect him to be a person of vitality, throwing himself with enthusiasm into the prosecution of his chosen life-plan and the myriad particular activities which it contains.

Virtues like these – prudence, courage, temperance, benevolence and the other moral virtues, lucidity, independence of mind, wisdom, humour and vitality – are the hallmarks of the educated man. This does not at all imply, of course, that the possession of knowledge or understanding, which other people sometimes make the hallmark, is not important. The educated man has to be knowledgeable in all sorts of ways. But for him knowledge is necessary to virtue: knowledgeableness is not a self-justifying state on its own.

The forms of knowledge or understanding he requires are indeed complex and extensive. I said something about them at the end of chapter 3, but since I had not then extended the notion of personal well-being to cover the moral concerns of chapters 4 and 5, a more comprehensive, if brief, specification is now appropriate.

The educated man will first have to understand in a general way what his own well-being consists in. This includes knowing something of the variety of ends-in-themselves which might be components of his life-plan, and something of the means he might adopt in achieving them, as well as obstacles to their achievement. Ends-in-themselves can be of all kinds. They include, among other things: enjoying physical pleasures, like eating, drinking, recreation; being esteemed by others, sociability; the enjoyment, production or performance of art; the pursuit of knowledge. Further subdivisions are possible within these and other categories: there are different foods, games, arts, forms of knowledge. How extensive and detailed we may expect the educated man's knowledge of ends to be is a difficult question. As we saw in chapter 3, there is a temptation to insist on too much, to demand a knowledge of all sub-sub-categories *ad infinitum*. This 'crazy comprehensiveness' was, we saw, the result of putting all the weight on one educational value – knowledge of ends – at the expense of others, like commitment to one's projects.

The truth in the theory that education should have intrinsic aims, discussed in chapter 2, should now be clearer. *One* element in a person's education should be an acquaintance with possible ends-in-themselves. But this kind of recommendation is not somehow self-justifying or intuitively known to be true. Its rationale comes from the total structure of the educational theory in which it is embedded: along with a number of other things, this kind of understanding is a *sine qua non* of the educated man as I have been delineating him. That version of the 'intrinsic' theory which says that the possession or pursuit of knowledge for its own sake is the stamp of educatedness is similarly not wholly false. The pursuit or possession of knowledge may indeed find a place among ends-in-themselves. But they are not the only such ends; nor is there reason to give them any priority among them. To do so would be badly to mislead one's pupils. But it is true, none the less, that a pupil who finishes up without any appreciation of, e.g. the pursuit of physical science or the history of art as a possible end-in-itself, has been seriously deprived.

We move from knowing ends to knowing means and obstacles. Means include both material necessary conditions – food, shelter, money, health, etc. – and self-regarding virtues like courage and temperance. I mentioned these virtues above. The point of introducing them here is that the educated man needs, as a part of *being* courageous and temperate, to *understand* why courage and temperance are important to him. Obstacles include psychological and socio-economic impediments among others. Generally, knowledge-objectives in this sphere of means and obstacles will cover, among other things, a good deal of understanding of the human sciences in general and their particular application to his situation in his society and in the world. Sociological, psychological, economic, political and geographical knowledge figure here. Clearly, too, more than a little historical knowledge is necessary to understand how the complex web of obstacles and opportunities which surrounds him has come to have the particular shape it does.

As well as knowing something about ends-in-themselves, means and obstacles, he needs to understand, more broadly, what personal well-being consists in, i.e. how these elements need to be integrated within an autonomous life-plan. This means he will have ideally to be something of a philosopher, able and prepared to think these things through without falling into obscurity or blindly taking over the pronouncements of authority. For this he will need both skills of clear thinking about such topics and some acquaintance with different traditions of thought, e.g. religious, about the good for man. This will require, in its turn, a broad understanding of different metaphysical pictures of the place of human life in the wider universe, not least of conflicts between theocentric pictures on the one hand and a naturalistic, evolution-based picture on the other.

The forms of knowledge outlined so far are – more or less – those dealt with at the end of chapter 3, when we were still working with our unextended concept of personal well-being. We have now to add those kinds he needs to have as a morally autonomous agent. Of course, all the forms of knowledge already discussed have a new relevance in this connexion: if he is concerned with others' well-being, he will not get very far without an understanding of what this well-being is in general and of the various constituents of this well-being, both intrinsic and instrumental. Actually *all* the kinds of knowledge he may require as a morally autonomous agent may be already covered under these headings. One might think that among the things one would have to add to these would be a knowledge of morality as an institution. But even from the most narrowly prudential of points of view this knowledge might well be advantageous to one. This aside, however, the moral demands on educatedness do throw into prominence the need for certain sorts of knowledge which might otherwise have been overlooked or played down: not only an understanding of morality − which again requires that our educated man have some at least embryonic philosophical leanings − but also insight into the situations in which the 'others' with whom he is morally connected find themselves and the conditions in which they are living. Once again, it is quite conceivable that some knowledge of, say, the widespread poverty in north-east Brazil could benefit even the meanest of egoists, but knowledge of this kind is more obviously a necessity for the broad-vista'd moral agent described in this chapter. Since 'others' may include people in his own society as well as those outside it − and, indeed, sentient non-human beings into the bargain − he will have to have a good deal of broad factual knowledge about them, drawn from such areas as sociology, human geography, international affairs, ecology. As a future worker, whose moral aspirations are expressed partly through the service he performs for others through his job, he needs to understand the possible moral significance of different forms of work. As a future citizen of a democracy both at state level and at local, or work-place, level, he will need knowledge both about the general principles of democratic organisation and about the particular applications of these principles to the specific situations in which he finds himself.

As a footnote to this sketch of the educated man, to forestall a possible misunderstanding, let me say something about the word 'life-plan', which has figured so prominently both in the sketch and in the earlier discussion. I do not wish to imply by it that the educated man is one who has drawn up a clear blueprint for how his life is to be lived with various stages and intermediate targets neatly mapped out. The word 'plan' may suggest such associations, but they are not what I intend. I mean something more general − that the educated man should have formed some kind of picture, in the light of all the considerations I have mentioned, about the kind of life he is to lead. This may well be something relatively inchoate, with broad outlines only, the details to be filled in as one goes, and even the broad outlines revisable if later reflection or changed circumstances warrant this. It *may* have more of the blueprint about it – I can see no reason for ruling this out as one option, but there is no necessity for this.

Problems of objectivity and indoctrination

This very brief delineation of the virtues and forms of understanding possessed by the educated man could be elaborated in all sorts of ways. If anything like this recommendation were ever taken up and applied to actual educational systems or institutions, it would *have* to be filled out, so that terminal objectives, e.g. of total school curricula, could be spelt out in more detail. Putting things like this might be thought to beg an important question. Is 'educatedness' a state which pupils leaving schools at 16 or 18 can be expected to possess? Or is it a more indeterminate quality? People talk and write these days about 'lifelong education' or 'l'éducation permanente'. If one accepts something like the components of educatedness just outlined, should one rather see them as achieved gradually, and then often never completely, over a whole lifetime?

I will return to these questions a little later. First, I want to tackle a fundamental objection to my account of the educated man which, if successful, would so completely undermine it that any further discussion of whether this kind of educatedness is achievable or not by the end of formal schooling would be a waste of time.

The objection is that my version of the educated man is, after all, only *my* version, reflecting my own, perhaps idiosyncratic and certainly culturally conditioned, value-judgments, which not all would share. If I am recommending that schools and other educational agencies follow some such set of aims, then by what right do I urge that they be *imposed* on children? Isn't my whole enterprise basically indoctrinatory, seeking to mould them into a certain pattern when the pattern itself is not beyond controversy? Why, in any case, should I lay such stress on uniformity? Why have educated men all got to be of the same type, all with identical qualities? Could we not reconceptualise things so that educators helped to produce educated men of widely differing sorts?

There are various kinds of anxiety expressed in these questions, but they are all to do with the justifiability of recommending one particular ideal. I think I can meet one of the objections – the one about uniformity – easily enough. Educated men will share a number of characteristics, but *precisely because they share them* they are likely to end up as persons with all sorts of different interests, values, points of view. They are alike in their autonomy, their self-directedness. This entails their having to strike their own balances in the many conflicts of value confronting them. Different individuals will strike different balances and choose different kinds of life-plan. We have no reason to think that this kind of education would produce any less variegatedness than say, the upbringing which most children in our own community currently receive. Today's children do not come to possess, for the most part, the broad-ranging knowledge about different life-options outlined here. Their conceptions about what sort of life they may lead are thus necessarily restricted. They are influenced, not surprisingly, by the conventional wisdom of their age. How many of them end up on the same conveyor-belts of values and attitudes, believing, for instance, that life is and can only be a competition for status, money, power, comfort? How many others, brought up within a religious framework, believe that life should consist in obedient execution of God's commands? How many girls grow up to think that their main role in life must be as mothers and housewives?

I can see no reason why the sort of educational aims I have been advocating should diminish the variety of ways of life: quite the contrary. Whether an education involving common, uniform aims for all children finishes up by making us carbon copies of each other depends on *what kind* of aims it involves. A religiously based education of a very strict and rigid kind, for instance, might well lead to this result. But where the only uniformity insisted on is that each person be an autonomous being, I can see no room for anxiety.

This will not allay all doubts about the proposals. Some people may be alarmed at the consequences of elevating dispositional aims above the possession of knowledge and understanding. To inculcate specific kinds of dispositions in children is to *mould* them into certain sorts of creature. Many have found it a great attraction of the 'liberal education'/ 'knowledge for its own sake' school of thought that its aim has not been to mould character but to liberate pupils from ignorance and misconceptions: it has often seemed the only educational route to take which avoids some kind of imposition or indoctrination.

But is it? It is not as though it avoids inculcating any disposition at all. It seeks to produce pupils with certain habits of mind: independence of thought, determination to find out the truth, lucidity and so on. But these are purely intellectual dispositions, it will be said. Implanting them cannot be indoctrinatory, because the more firmly pupils acquire them, the more inclined they will be to reflect on and possibly reject ideas which others have passed on to them. This is not so, it will be argued, when it comes to moral dispositions. They are not anti-indoctrinatory in their essence. Bringing children up to be honest, considerate, tolerant, benevolent is moulding their characters in such a way that they *stay* people of this sort. The liberal educationist may even go so far as to want his pupils to reach that degree of intellectual autonomy which allows them to reject that autonomy if they so wish: he may say it is all the same to him if a pupil of his decides to become a religious believer taking things henceforth on authority alone. (Whether he *would* go as far as this would depend on what his view of a liberal education allowed.)

It is now not so clear just what is wrong with 'moulding' children in moral virtues. Indoctrination is objectionable in general because the indoctrinated person is prevented from reflecting upon and thence possibly rejecting beliefs that he has had implanted in him or that he possesses already. A liberal education is anti-indoctrinatory in its encouragement of independent-mindedness, even possibly to the extent of questioning the virtue of independent-mindedness itself and possibly rejecting it to become a religious believer. If we spell things out like this, however, it is no longer clear what is indoctrinatory about 'moulding' children in morality. We can teach them to be honest and considerate without wanting to prevent them reflecting on the attendant beliefs that they should be virtuous in these ways. True, we *might* mould them in an indoctrinatory way. Children are sometimes brought up to believe it is morally right to be obedient to authority and morally wrong to disobey; and very often the last thing their teachers want them to do is to think about whether obedience is really justified. But this is not the only form of moral education: we could leave children free to think about the virtues we are inculcating into them, or even positively encourage them to do this.

'But it's not much good their thinking about the justifiability of considerateness if they've been so moulded that they can't help being considerate', an objector may point out.

The basic question is by what right does one do the moulding? Why select the virtues one does? What justification can one give to show that one is not simply passing on values prized in our particular culture, but perhaps not elsewhere? More generally, why inculcate *moral* virtues at all? Morality is a commitment. It's not the sort of thing that any rational being *must* accept: the amoral egoist may always be able to defend the rationality of his position. So when we are making children into moral beings, we are committing them to a way of life which is not justifiable up to the hilt.

Again, there are a number of different objections here. I agree that there are dangers in inculcating dispositions which help to imprison children within the way of life of a particular culture, since this is at odds with the ideal of autonomy I have been arguing for. It has been traditional in our own culture to bring up girls to be submissive creatures in a male-dominated society; and in some sub-cultures, e.g. Moslem, within our own, there has been an even stricter insistence on this alleged virtue. If we want *all* our children to grow up into autonomous beings, we must counteract the social forces which steer girls into a submissive role from birth onwards. This is not to depreciate *all* dispositions of a culturally conditioned sort. Children have to grow up within particular cultures and within a framework of mores of a concrete and cashable sort. So if English children are brought up with sets of table-manners or politeness-rules which vary considerably from those of, say, Indian or Japanese children, I see no harm in that as long as in none of these cases they are hindered in their development as autonomous beings.

What, though, if the autonomy ideal is itself culturally conditioned? In one sense it is, of course. It is not a universal feature of all cultures. Historically, it goes back perhaps little further than the seventeenth century; geographically, there are large tracts of the world today which would not countenance it, not least those dominated by Catholicism, Islam and many forms of Communism. But the central question is whether it is *objectively valid*, i.e. such that we can say that even though children in Paraguay or Saudi Arabia are not in fact brought up to be autonomous, nevertheless there are good reasons why they *ought* to be.

To argue for the objectivity of the autonomy ideal would be to repeat the case I have built up for it thus far in the book. It would mean going into what the good of the individual consists in, first in the unextended and then in the extended sense. There is nothing in that whole stretch of argument which should lead anyone to think it applicable only to education in Britain or in 'western culture'. This is obviously not the place to go through all those points again. It is true that if some of them are importantly wrong, the theory would have to be revised before it was used to back any practical recommendations. But that need not be grounds for dismissing it completely, rather than, say, for patching up particular defects while keeping much of its main structure. What, if anything, needs to be altered I must leave it to the reader to judge.

One last point. I have not claimed that there will be complete agreement on all sides about the aims I have put forward. If uncontroversiality is a necessary condition of objectivity, then I could not pretend this has been an objective account. But it *isn't* a necessary condition. Some people still believe the earth is flat, but I can still state objectively that it is not. In any case, if we were to insist on universal consensus before accepting any educational aims, I doubt whether we would get anywhere. Not even literacy would get *everybody's* vote. Near-consensus would give us a highest common factor of the so-called 'basic skills' but precious little else. Would it then be rational to aim *only* at teaching the basic skills? No more, I think, than to insist that the state should concern itself only with external affairs and law and order because this is the area which all political parties would agree on.

One person who would not accept the aims in this book would be the amoralist, the complete egoist to whom morality is pointless or unintelligible. If this man asks me for a justification of moulding children in moral virtues like considerateness, I do not know that I can give him one that will be foolproof against all possible objections. But how much should that worry me? Just because one cannot rationally convince a psychopath of one's beliefs, should one give them up? I readily admit that justifications cannot go on for ever and that somewhere one reaches bedrock commitments. I am taking it for granted, as I said earlier, that my readers will agree with me that men should not attend only to their own well-being but be concerned with others' as well. At this point I appeal not to further, knock-down reasons, but to fundamental attitudes about human life which I am taking it we all share.

Childhood education and lifelong education

To return to the 'educated man' and the different kinds of dispositions and knowledge or understanding which he possesses. How far can one begin to translate these into terminal objectives for school systems? How far can we now set about deciding what pupils ought minimally to know and what kinds of dispositions they should have acquired, by the age of, say, 16 or so when they finish compulsory schooling? If we *can* work out terminal objectives of this sort, then we can provide a framework within which subordinate objectives may be temporally laid out, so that the whole period of compulsory schooling, from 5 to 16, can be seen as a continuous whole, with sub-objectives for children at different ages or stages and, at the very detailed level, particular courses for specific years or terms planned out in line with the sub-objectives. I make no comment here about what role the teacher, as opposed to central or local government, should have in determining these objectives and sub-objectives. That is another question. The one which interests me here is to what extent the outline of educational aims given here can help us to determine a broad framework for the content of school education as a necessary condition of rational planning at subordinate levels.

On the plus side, I hope at least I have done enough to rebut the kind of critic who says that theorising about educational aims is a waste of time because it must remain at such a level of abstraction and vagueness as to be uncashable in any way that might help the work of schools. In discussing aims, we need not remain for ever at the level of 'happiness' or 'individuality' or even 'autonomy'. We *can* spell out more specific implications, as witness the burgeoning description of dispositions and forms of understanding at the beginning of this chapter, a description which could well be filled out in all sorts of more specific ways.

Against this, one has to put the fact that schooling is only *one* way in which educational aims may be realised. If it were the only way, then the move from aims to terminal objectives to sub-objectives could be made quite smoothly. But since it isn't, a logical gap immediately opens up between aims and terminal school objectives. What we need to know is what place the school should have among the various institutions or other agencies which can help to realise educational aims. Only then will we be in a position to work out *its* objectives *vis-à-vis* the contributions made elsewhere.

What these other institutions and agencies might be is the topic of the next and final chapter, on the realisation of aims. But in order to proceed to that, we need to look a bit further into the concept of educatedness. When does the pupil become educated? At what point in his life are the aims of his education realised? Is it at 'maturity', however this is to be understood? Or is it wrong to think of educatedness in this way as a state to be achieved still fairly early in one's life? If education is to be reconceptualised as a 'lifelong process' and not as something belonging only to youth, then we might as well drop the concept of the educated man: there is no line to be crossed; the journey goes on for ever.

All this bears on the topic of the next chapter. If education belongs wholly or mainly to youth, then certain agencies, not least the home and the school, become salient. If it is lifelong and the period of youth has no priority, other means may become more prominent.

So what are we to say about 'educatedness'? The word and its cognates can be used in different ways. In this book I have taken 'education' very broadly to mean 'upbringing', arguing for a certain kind of upbringing, directed towards certain ends and not others. Whenever this education ends, there should be no doubt about when it begins. It begins in infancy and continues at least through childhood. It is not something that can be put off entirely until one's adult years. Every child must have some sort of upbringing. I shall take this as obvious. Equally obvious is that the main outlines of a person's character are formed in his early years. It is in childhood that one learns gradually not to tell lies, to refrain from hurting others, to bear pain or disappointment, and so on. I do not know whether it is conceivable that these and other dispositions be only acquired in adulthood; but if it is logically possible, we can safely say, I think, that it is psychologically incredible. If so, the main girders of the kind of education I am recommending will have to be put in place in the early years. If education were seen in a different way, as concerned, for instance, with the pursuit of knowledge or aesthetic enjoyment for its own sake, then the early years would lack this priority. Childhood could (although it need not) be seen as a period of preparation for education, education itself taking place in adulthood. On the present view of education, however, things could not be like that.

Much of the framework of a person's conceptual schemes must also be built up early on. Children cannot be left until they are 18 or 20 before they learn language. Neither can they be deprived of experience of the natural and human world around them so as to postpone their acquiring concepts and information about these matters until they are grown up. Children need to make some sort of sense of their world and it is rational to try to ensure that they don't get things wildly wrong. Hence one good reason for not postponing the whole of intellectual learning, any more than dispositional learning, until adulthood. In both spheres the main lines have to be laid down when young.

All this would be platitudinous, were it not for the widespread interest, inspired by the prospect of a new leisure-age, in 'life-long education'. Clive Jenkins, on 'Any Questions?' an hour or so ago, was urging us to think of education not as a preparation for life but as a way of life. This is a popular way of talking, but it might lead to confusion. Whatever else happens, there must be some sort of preparation for life in any society. If you prefer to call it 'upbringing' rather than 'education' I don't mind: the important thing is the concept, not the word. An essential feature of upbringing is that it is not a voluntary process for the child. He cannot choose whether or not he is brought up. Upbringing is necessarily something imposed on him. If one adopts the aims I have outlined, his upbringing will make him free to make his own choices. This is what it is about. But to become free, he must pass through a period of compulsory education (in the 'upbringing' sense).

'Lifelong education' or 'education as a way of life' is importantly different from upbringing. It is usually seen as, and is only morally defensible as, a voluntary undertaking. In the new leisure society people will be free to spend a large part of their time in learning. What sort of things they learn as part of their lifelong education depends on what is built into this concept. It may embrace only activities pursued for their own sake, or more narrowly, the pursuit of knowledge for its own sake. It may also cover practical skills involved in occupational retraining. But whatever the content, it is normally taken to be voluntary. Its supporters talk of rights and opportunities, not of compulsion. And this is only morally right. If an adult states that he does not want to be made to keep on studying, is there any valid reason to insist that he does? It might well be that most people in the leisure society will want to learn things anyway, and where learning activities occupy a large fraction of their time we may well want to talk of education being (in their case, not necessarily in others') a way of life. But there are other things one can do in one's life than learning − gardening, for instance, playing games, making love, cakes or conversation. Some people may go for these more than for new sorts of learning.

The danger, in saying that we must think of education no longer as a preparation for life but as a way of life or at least as lifelong, is that we might blur the vital distinction between a person's upbringing, which for him cannot be voluntary, and his adult learning activities, whether cultural or occupational, which should be voluntary. Both of these are important, and I do not deny that the second may well be increasingly prominent in the future. But there should be no question of shifting the emphasis from one to the other. Whatever happens, upbringing is a *sine qua non*.

While sound in its broad outlines, the distinction just made is still rather too crude. We begin to see this if we return to the original question: when does education as I have been outlining it end? At what stage in his life can we say that a man has become educated?

The quick answer would be: when he has acquired the dispositions and forms of understanding specified in the aims. But this would be too quick. For both these things can be possessed *in different degrees.* One can be more, or less, thoughtful, lucid, courageous. One may understand quite a lot, or quite a little, about the variety of possible ends-in-themselves, means-to-ends, obstacles and so on. *How much* are we to demand of the educated man?

Only the broadest outlines are clear. The extent of the learning minimally required of him must be determined by the demands of the autonomy ideal in its extended sense. In the area of ends-in-themselves, for instance, it would not do if he knew nothing about the different art-forms, since this would restrict him in his choice of a life-plan. But it would be too much to require that he be acquainted with, say, Ravel's String Quartet: one might have to know some musical works, but not necessarily this one.

We might be able to indicate an area in each of the major forms of learning which is neither too little nor too much. But the area would still often be very indeterminate. Sometimes, it is true, it would be less so. Truthfulness is a virtue where differences of degree should not come into the reckoning. We rightly expect children to learn *always* to tell the truth, unless they judge that this is overridable, in exceptional instances, by some other moral principle.

But what are we to say about their need to integrate their ends and means within a morally acceptable plan of life? What would count as a minimum *here*? We may well be tempted, once we reflect on the difficulties, to conclude that the distinction between education as upbringing and lifelong education must break down at this point. For integration is *never* complete. Our priorities change throughout our lives, partly through reflection on incoherencies in our life-plan, for instance, and partly through changing circumstances – marriage, a family, sickness, growing older, becoming richer or poorer, changing one's job, world economic conditions etc. – which force revaluations upon us. So if the educated man is someone who has a fully integrated life-plan, he cannot be 20 years old, or 30 or even 40. His education, in my sense, must go on throughout his life. The only satisfactory upbringing *is* lifelong education.

While there is a lot which is true and important in this point of view, it is, even so, an exaggeration. It would seem to imply, for instance, that the 80-year-old man who is readjusting his priorities in the light of old age still has not completed his upbringing. We need not go so far as this, but can argue instead that a person is more or less educated – and there is nothing at all precise about this – when he has formed something like a coherent life-plan in the light of all the considerations built into the substantive account of educational aims presented earlier, and is aware of the kinds of future circumstances which might cause him to adjust his valuations as he goes through life. This is still rather vague, I agree, but it is perhaps just sufficiently determinate to make it possible to call, say, a 30-year-old man brought up on the lines suggested in this book more or less 'educated'.

It will be understood that this is only an indication. I am not taking thirty, or any other age, as cut-off point. This is partly because there are no sharp lines, only very blurred areas, in anybody's case; and partly because people learn at different rates and some may be slower than others in reaching the blurred area. Some may never reach it, although we may still want to call them partially educated, since they have travelled some way along the same road as others.

How does all this relate to the earlier point that upbringing is not voluntary for the pupil? It shows, I think, that that view is too crude as it stands and needs qualification. Talk of a 'blurred area' in which the state of educatedness is reached means that whatever good reasons exist – and they do exist – for insisting on certain learning objectives up to the boundaries of that blurred area become weaker once the pupil is inside that area: if at that point he claims the right not to receive further education, he is on obviously stronger ground than before he reached it.

A second consideration is this. There may be a conflict between two principles, the principle that everyone ought to become an educated person, and the principle that every adult ought to be left free to conduct his own life as he sees fit unless he is doing harm to others or, in some circumstances, to himself. The conflict could arise if, say, a particular person would not reach the blurred area, if he reached it at all, until he was, say, 30. Should one insist that he remain in tutelage until that time? The principle of universal educatedness pulls us in that direction, but the principle of universal liberty pulls against. One might reply that the principle of liberty is not unqualified: if liberty can be overridden on the grounds of harm to others or oneself, then we might have a good reason for insisting on his being educated until aged 30 – if, for instance, we can show that his being insufficiently educated is harmful in these ways. But it is perhaps not enough to show that *some* harm will result. People are not *prevented* from eating too much fatty food, even though they might be restrained from playing with a loaded revolver when drunk. One has to weigh the degree of harm in the balance. Only if great harm (however one defines this) will result from a person's not becoming fully educated has one got a clear moral reason for keeping him at school or its equivalent until 30. Perhaps in some cases, e.g. of psychopathy considered to be remediable, society would be justified in, e.g., detaining people until that age in institutions where such educational work could go on. But in many other cases the claims of liberty may weigh more heavily.

These two considerations – the existence of a blurred area and of the countervailing principle of liberty – make it reasonable to draw a distinction between the end of compulsory education and the achievement of educatedness. For some pupils the two may coincide: by the end of the compulsory period they may already be educated. A few exceptional individuals may reach this target even before this time. In their case there might be good reason to waive any legal requirement that they be kept at school, say, for another year or two.

Most pupils are unlikely, perhaps, to be educated when they finish compulsory education. (I have not said when this compulsory period should end. In practice, there are often financial and other constraints which determine it. It is 16 in this country at the moment. Is this about right? How would one determine it if these constraints were absent?) The principle of liberty forbids us to compel them beyond a certain (not very precise) point, but the principle of educatedness equally forbids us to do *nothing* for them beyond this point. If it is a good thing that they become educated, we have a strong reason to *encourage*, but not compel them in that direction. This goes a little further than saying that post-compulsory provision should exist on a voluntary basis. It could mean, for instance, providing incentives in time or money for young workers to undertake educational courses or to pursue their own self-education. It could mean reshaping conventional social expectations via the media, for instance, so that becoming educated in the full sense becomes the done thing. It could mean not only strengthening and making more accessible those agencies – careers guidance units, marriage counsellors, almoners, Gingerbread groups, Cruse, psychiatric services and so on – which can help people to reflect on the shape of their lives as a whole (sometimes after the disruption of e.g. a serious illness, divorce or bereavement), but also reconceptualising them as *educational* agencies. Looked at this way, the period of compulsory education would have the function of laying the groundwork for a coherent life-plan, with strong encouragement for the individual after this period to reconsider and revise this life-plan with help from formal and informal agencies, if necessary.

By 'the end of compulsory education' I do not necessarily mean 'the end of schooling'. The school-leaving age in this country is currently fixed at 16. But as early as the First World War there was legislation (in the 1918 Education Act) to introduce compulsory part-time continuation education until 18. This was shelved in the economic cuts after that war, but it provides a possible model for us to consider today. We might then envisage compulsory full-time schooling until say 16 or later, possibly followed by compulsory part-time education for another period, with strong official encouragement to continue one's education on a voluntary basis beyond that point. This would not be 'lifelong' education, since the overall objective would only be to produce educated persons and this might be achievable while people are still young. Still further provision for voluntary adult education and work-retraining for later age-groups could be tacked on to this basic educational programme, but its objectives, important though they are, should not be confused with the latter's.

Different aims for different pupils?

The earlier sketch of the educated man took it as read that educatedness is the same for all pupils. Lying behind this assumption has been the principle that, in distributing goods, one should not treat people differently unless there are relevant grounds for discriminating between them. At several points earlier in the book I have looked at suggestions that aims should vary: suggestions about the leisure-class and excellence in chapter 2; the encouragement of individual differences, in chapter 3; and Platonic conceptions of education for citizenship in chapter 5. In no case did there seem a cogent case for discrimination.

The strongest appeals against a universal set of aims are those based on ability on the one hand and resources on the other. As regards ability, I know of no evidence that the demands of educatedness are pitched so high here that the overwhelming majority of pupils cannot reach them, given their period of compulsory schooling is planned as a unified whole, and given compensatory, especially pre-school, education for those who need it. I have stressed that educatedness is a state with very blurred boundaries, so that not all may be expected to leave the system as fully educated as others, even though they all reach some kind of basic minimum. Arguments against common aims based on alleged differences of ability I have, by and large, rejected. Ceilings-arguments would be powerful here, if one could show that some pupils' intellectual ceilings were so low that they could not achieve the relatively modest objectives implicit in educatedness. I have argued already against the doctrine of ceilings.

Where I am least confident that the aims should be the same for all children without exception is in the area of severe mental sub-normality. The Warnock Report on *Special Educational Needs* (HMSO, 1978) insists that 'the purpose of education for all children is the same; the goals are the same' (1.4). This is in spite of the admission that for some children one of the main goals – becoming an active participant in society after leaving school – 'may never be achieved' (*ibid.*). I find this muddling. It might be less confusing to allow a breach in the principle of universal aims at least for the small percentage of children whose disabilities are so great that they cannot, say, learn to speak, and perhaps for other children besides. (Whether the ceilings-argument applies to the most disabled children is an interesting question. These children *do* seem to have ceilings, in that, owing, for example to brain-damage, attempts to get them to learn invariably fail. Of course, the next attempt may always in principle succeed. But there is a limit to how far one can vary one's teaching with a language-less child. With normal, language-possessing children, there are infinitely more variations one can try. This is why the ceilings-argument seems so much less applicable to them.) This need not imply that the aims of *education* may vary. One could hold, instead, that the most severely handicapped children are ineducable. I do not propose to take a stand on this issue. What does seem reasonable is that the aims proposed in this book are probably not applicable to *all* children, but only, at most, to *virtually all* children.

Can one make further inroads into the universality principle if one turns to the other end of the ability range? Is educatedness, as so described, sufficient for the very quick or talented pupil? Although I have looked at related issues in the discussion of excellence in chapter 2 and elsewhere, I am aware that many people will still have serious reservations, and often weighty ones. Sometimes the proposition that education should have common aims is taken to imply that all children should be taught by the same procedures or in classes where they are all learning the same thing at the same time. Mixed-ability teaching is sometimes organised in this way and for this reason. Parents and others then tend to complain that quicker children are being held back. They often go on from that to espouse the view that there should be different kinds of education for children of different abilities leading to different objectives. But the protagonists and antagonists in this debate share the illicit assumption that what goes for aims goes also for implementation at classroom level: common aims go with common lessons, different lessons with different aims. There is no reason why the two should go together. One can readily agree that quicker or more knowledgeable children sometimes need different fare from others: for one thing, one cannot, logically, learn what one already knows and if we accept it as desirable that every child keeps on learning things, it makes little sense regularly to have a child who already knows X in a class where X is the learning-objective, unless some kind of special provision is made for him to work for some other proximate goal. Much mixed-ability teaching is, of course, based on individualised learning in this latter way. But believing that children should not be held back does not imply setting different ultimate aims for them. There are at least two ways in which their work may be contained within the same framework of aims. The first is by allowing them to finish their compulsory education early once they are within the target area of educatedness. I raised this possibility earlier in the chapter. This might or might not go together with a system of speeded-up promotion through year-groups. The second way is by laying on plenty of voluntary activities outside the compulsory educational system, so that those who want to learn more about chemistry, history or whatever than the compulsory system includes, or want to learn things, e.g. how to play the harp, which are not part of the compulsory programme at all, have an opportunity to do so. (This is only one reason in favour of a voluntary system, about which I shall be saying more below.)

Differences in ability are not the only ground on which differences of aim have been supported. Scarcity of resources is another. Suppose a very poor country in the Third World were setting up an educational system. It might be too poor to bring all up to the minimum level of educatedness suggested above, able only to afford this for say, 20 per cent of the population. In these circumstances, at least except for the very long term, education might have to be reserved only for an elite. (I say 'might': there is a lot more that would have to be argued through before one was in a position to say anything more categorical.) If Britain (say) were also a country in which resources were too scarce to allow universal educatedness, one might have to say the same. Some people, indeed, do say this, supporting a selective system for just this reason. But this looks like special pleading. We already invest several billion pounds per annum in education at all levels. If our aims were clearer and there were more co-ordination between different parts of the system, we might come nearer the mark even without increasing the amount spent on the school system. Later, in chapter 7, I shall be arguing, in effect, that a lot of what happens in undergraduate university teaching is not really educational: if more resources are needed for the schools – and for pre-school provision – there is a strong case for siphoning them off from 'higher education' (see pp. 163–4). Quite apart from these realignments of priorities within the overall education budget and from possible reallocations within government expenditure as a whole, e.g. from defence to education, if yet more resources are necessary, I am not convinced that Britain is too poor to provide it. Last Saturday I spent an absorbing but tiring afternoon looking around Ferdinand de Rothschild's art-treasures and other possessions at Waddesdon in Bucks, a house now belonging to the National Trust. Up and down the country there are hundreds of Waddesdons still in private hands, thousands of lesser Waddesdons and millions of mimesis-spawned miniscule Waddesdons. We are not short of private wealth, whether in property or in bank accounts. If we wanted to use some of it to help to give everyone a good basic education, the resources are there all right. Whether everyone would want them to be so used is, of course, another matter.

Chapter 7

The realisation of aims

A reasonably full account of how educational aims are to be realised in practice would embrace a large part of educational theory, both general and subject-specific, and more besides. I cannot hope to embark on this here. But I do not wish to leave the discussion wholly in the air without any indications at all of how it might be brought closer to the ground. Indications are indeed all I shall have space for, the bare outline of a larger picture. Some will find this unsatisfactory, as it is the practicalities which in the last analysis are of central importance: what use is it to have even a valid and attractive set of aims unless one knows in some detail how to translate them into reality? I agree absolutely. All the most vital work still remains to be done. This analysis is at most a prolegomenon. But some kind of prolegomenon is essential.

There may indeed be some advantage in only being able to give a bare sketch of the larger picture. For this should draw attention to its structural features, its main elements. It will help us to tackle the practical problems from as broad a perspective as possible, thus being less likely to ignore certain ways of trying to achieve our educational ends just because we have approached the topic on too narrow a front. Illustrations of this point will appear below.

Socio-economic conditions

The central aim of education, I have argued, ought to be that the pupil becomes a morally autonomous person. The realisation of this aim depends on various kinds of necessary conditions. First and most obviously, it requires certain capabilities, understanding and dispositions in the pupil himself. But it requires other things too. It will only be achievable in a society living above the level of bare subsistence, with adequate material provision, health and educational services, good

140

working conditions and leisure opportunities for all. There may, in other words, be economic and other necessary conditions, over and above the intellectual and other achievements of the pupil. This is perhaps a banal point in itself, but it reinforces something stressed more than once in earlier chapters, that teachers (including parents) should not see their work as self-contained, cut off from the wider life of society. As teachers, their prime contribution to the overall aim of education will naturally be to do with their pupils' capacities and dispositions. But if they are seriously concerned about this overall aim they should also care about its other, e.g. economic, necessary conditions. It follows from this that an interest in education should not be divorced from an interest in politics.

This provides a first illustration of the claim I made just now, that a schematic picture of how aims are to be realised should help to prevent narrowness. It is natural and right for teachers to think especially about the necessary conditions with which they are professionally concerned, i.e. the states of mind of the pupil. But it is not right for them *only* to consider these, since there may also be necessary conditions not essentially connected with pedagogy which they should take into account. They should do so, too, not only as *teachers* but also as *citizens*. The ordinary citizen who is not a teacher (again, 'teacher' here includes 'parent') may well have nothing directly to do with forming capacities or dispositions, but he may help to promote educational aims by political or other activity. The teacher has *both* routes open to him. (He can, of course, see part of his specifically pedagogic work as equipping his pupils with capacities which will help to bring about some of the non-pedagogic necessary conditions: in a developing society, for instance, a sounder knowledge of agriculture across the population may help to raise it above the level of bare subsistence; and in our own society schools can play a part in maintaining and strengthening our economic base.)

Educational means

Given adequate socio-economic conditions, what educational means are available to promote the aims suggested?

(1) *The ethos of the community*
One answer lies in the ethos of the whole community, quite apart from the particular contribution of the school and its curriculum. Social

institutions in general can help to shape the consciousness and moral character of individuals – an insight associated first with the Greeks and, in modern times, with Hegel and Marx. A community's laws, its political system, its press, its industrial organisation, the mores of its family and neighbourhood life – these and others besides are all potentially educative forces, for good or ill.

If we look for a moment at our own society, it is clear that much will have to be done to improve its institutions if they are to work towards and not against the kind of educational aims I have proposed. At a very general level, influential moralities, like the authoritarian codes of many religious people, or the moral minimalism castigated in chapter 4, are obviously at odds with them. There may be ways, other than through formal educational institutions, of trying to combat them. Literature, for instance, can be a powerful weapon: witness the success of Dickens's literary campaign against mid-nineteenth-century greed and hard-heartedness. A more humane moral awareness on the part of newspaper editors and journalists, television producers and scriptwriters would also help: too many of them pander too often to conventional moralities, not least minimalism. Whether this can come about by internal reforms within the media or only by putting external controls on them is difficult to say.

There is much more that could be said about general moral attitudes, but, since this is only a sketch, let us turn now to more specific beliefs often associated with them. One deep-rooted assumption in our society is that those of greater intellectual achievements should have a larger income than others. There is no rational basis for this: it has just come to be the convention. Its anti-educational influence is not hard to see: schoolchildren, pressed on by their parents, work hard at school so as to pass their O and A levels in the prospect of a well-paid job. The aims of their education, as I argued in earlier chapters, are misplaced.

A second piece of conventional wisdom is that work-institutions should be hierarchically arranged, with those above telling those immediately below them what to do. This message, reinforced at every end and turn, is at odds with the demands of personal autonomy. As with the ability/income example, it is an ill-organised society in which the attitudes which schools laboriously build up are flatly contradicted by the way in which work-places are organised.

A third example is the consumer-centred picture of the good life that industry, advertising and the mass media together portray. Children learn that it is a good thing to have a lot of material possessions; that it is good to possess what is currently in fashion; that marginal differences between goods in the same range are of great significance. In my earlier discussion of personal well-being I said nothing to *rule out* pupils' giving a high priority to things of this sort: whether or not they go for this is finally up to them. But what is alarming is just how difficult it is for them to escape the pressure to adopt this view, either from television or from their families or from the playground. It is anti-educational that so particular a picture of the good life should be allowed such domination: it conflicts with the demand that the pupil autonomously chooses his way of life from a wide range of alternatives, since many alternatives are in danger of being blotted out.

To try to ensure that it does not work against the aims of education, the ethos of our community in these and no doubt other of its manifestations needs to be redirected. The tie between ability and income needs to be severed and some more rational system of income-distribution introduced. Jobs for which higher intellectual achievements are currently required are usually among the more interesting: if they carried less income than they do now, those qualified would probably prefer to do them anyway. There is a good case for so arranging the rewards that different jobs bring – not only monetary rewards but those also of leisure and intrinsic satisfactions – that all jobs ideally help to promote the personal well-being in its extended sense which has figured so prominently in our educational aims, with arduous and unpleasant jobs generating far more leisure, for instance, than those with high intrinsic satisfactions. This would be a far cry from a society where some people, often the most intellectually qualified, get jobs with substantial rewards in every category and others have to make do – if they are employed at all – with low-paid, unpleasant work which leaves them little leisure. If we are to take the educational aims in this book seriously, we will have to improve the lot of those in the second group.

To combat the threat to personal, including moral, autonomy posed by the hierarchical arrangement of work-places, a move to more democratic regimes is essential. It would take too long to explain what I mean by a 'democratic regime', but a central feature of it is that it goes beyond a representative system of national or local government in which 90-odd per cent of the electorate are politically inactive except on the rare occasions when they vote, towards a more fully participatory democracy, in which day-to-day sharing in decision-making is a normal part of life. A participatory democracy, unlike a merely representative one, would necessitate the democratisation of work and other institutions in which individuals co-exist face to face, since it is only at this level, in large-scale state communities at least, that day-to-day decision-making is found. A participatory democracy could help to educate the community by enlarging the understanding of its participants about the enterprises in which they work and encouraging them in habits of autonomous moral decision-making. I am assuming in this that the industrial democracy envisaged will not be premised, as the traditional organisation of industry has been premised, on narrowly economic objectives, but will see industry and the media as means of bringing about a wider communal well-being.

Ways, too, should be found of counteracting the privileged position of the high-consumption, fashion-oriented ideal of life. I do not have any very determinate idea of what might be done, although reforms made in income distribution and in the democratisation of work may help here, too, the first by helping to lessen the salience of monetary wealth in pictures of the good life, the second by putting the people who work in the mass media and advertising less under the thumb of industrial entrepreneurs, making them more publicly accountable and in a better position to shape their work to ends which they can morally justify.

These are only three examples among many of ways in which the social ethos may be brought more in line with educational aims. Each of them may or may not involve legislative action, but they all require at all events some kind of political engagement. What all this underlines is, as before, that educational progress should not be seen as something self-contained, to do only with schools, teachers and pupils: it is intimately connected with larger improvements in our industrial, political and other social institutions. This is a more specific demand than the similar one made at the beginning of this chapter. There I was reminding parents and schoolteachers that they should be interested in what happens in industry because there are material as well as pedagogical conditions to be satisfied if educational aims are to be realised. Here I am saying that there is a further reason for this interest even if one restricts oneself to the pedagogical conditions. In other words, if teachers aim at the intellectual and moral achievements in their pupils which I have advocated, it is less than rational of them to take no interest in what other institutions could do to help bring about the same end. Teachers today often, and rightly, complain that the competitive, utilitarian ethos of industrial society is directly at odds with the attitudes they are trying to foster in school. But it is no answer to cut oneself off still further from the alien world outside, seeing the school as a besieged citadel of truth, beauty and goodness in a society intent on destroying these. If their own work is not to come to nothing as their pupils become increasingly affected by the mores of that society, teachers have a special duty not merely to take a lively interest in public affairs, but also to adopt a certain political *line*. They should support any moves to shift the social ethos away from its anti-educational values. This is not necessarily to say that they must be left-wingers rather than right-wingers. But it *is* to say that no teacher can bury himself in his world of real numbers or the works of Thomas Hardy and claim that politics should be kept out of education.

(2) *Schools*

Whenever I address teacher audiences these days, about the need to change school curricula in various ways, I always provoke the challenge from one or two people in the audience that 'You can't change schools without changing society.' It may seem that the drift of my remarks above is in line with this familiar tag. It is so only to a point. It is true that it is not *enough* to change schools: society must be changed as well. But it does not follow that there is *no point* in trying to change schools on the grounds that schools necessarily reflect society and so the only way to bring about a change in schools is by a full-scale political revolution for which all teachers must work. On that argument, no particular social institution can be reformed before the whole society is revolutionised. And this can lead swiftly to the conclusion that until the revolution happens, we had better leave things as they are. What else, after all, can we do? We can find, moreover, good Marxist authority for not changing the *status quo*: if the old order is to be overturned, it must be ripe to be so. The contradictions within it must be left to work themselves out and thoroughly undermine it; only then can the revolution give it its final *coup de grâce*: all of which helps to explain the conservatism noticeable among so many Marxist educationists.

Changing schools can be one way of helping to realise the aims of education. It should be matched with other social changes, in the structure of industry and elsewhere. But even if progress elsewhere is slow or non-existent, this does not mean that schools can do nothing on their own. Only if a very strong version of social determinism were true could this be ruled out, but no good arguments for it seem available. Schools can help to achieve educational aims in two ways, by their ethos and by their courses of study, their curricula.

Before turning to those, however, I would like to say something about how the general arguments about aims in this book relate specifically to the school system operating in England and Wales, as we know it today. Until very recently – and still now in some quarters – we have had a selective system in which different aims have been envisaged for children in different types of secondary school. Grammar schools have been very largely in the 'knowledge for its own sake' tradition, although all those connected with them – parents, teachers and pupils alike – have been aware, to differing degrees, of the vocational advantages of high academic achievement, the university education to which it can lead on being an entrée to a professional career. Secondary-modern schools have had less clearly defined aims. There has been some pressure to mould them, like the elementary schools they superseded, into instruments of 'gentling' the large majority of children into accepting manual or other lowly vocations, both by orienting curricula towards practical or industrial pursuits and by instituting an ethos of submissiveness to authority which has fitted hand-in-glove with companies' requirements. At the same time more humane influences have been at work, calling for intrinsic rather than instrumental ends, but intrinsic ends like the pursuit of practical aesthetic activities of different sorts, allegedly more within the capacities of the secondary-modern child than the academic work of the grammar school. A third influence has been the schools' attempts to overcome their image of second-rateness by aping the grammar schools. So the aims, already described, of the grammar schools have come to affect the work of the secondary moderns also.

As for primary schools, these have tended to be pulled in one or both of two directions. Some people have seen their central task as laying a firm foundation in the 'basics'; for others it has been to allow the child's individuality to blossom. Neither aim has necessarily been incompatible with the existence of a selective system after 11.

Alongside state schools, independent, including public, schools have co-existed. Here, as in grammar schools, knowledge-for-its-own-sake has been a prominent aim, along with the vocational aims with which this tends to get entangled. Education for leadership has also been an important feature, especially via non-curricular activities or the 'hidden curriculum'.

This is only a very crude sketch of what, examined in detail, is no doubt a bewilderingly complicated reality. It leaves out, for one very important thing, the religious aims of various sorts which pervade the work of schools of all kinds.

Comprehensive schools have grown up among this welter of different aims. To a large extent they have been coloured by what has gone on before – not surprisingly, since many of them have been amalgams of grammar and secondary-modern schools and have drawn their staff from teachers long used to a selective system. In many comprehensives this system has in effect been perpetuated under one roof. At the same time other comprehensives have sought to work out for themselves and for others new sets of aims more in line with the egalitarian and other principles which helped to generate the idea of comprehensive education in the first place. In many cases the directions in which these have been moving – away from divided towards common aims, away from an overpreoccupation with knowledge for its own sake and towards personal autonomy and equipment for democratic participation at different levels – are the directions also of this book. If the latter can help especially, but not only, the comprehensive teacher in working out new sets of aims of these sorts it will have served its purpose. (I must be careful here. I said something similar in my earlier book, *Towards a Compulsory Curriculum*, which I was bold – and brash – enough to offer to the world as a guideline for a left-wing curriculum policy; but the only politician who corresponded with me about it and seemed to like it was Sir Keith Joseph.)

(a) *Ethos*

I do not want to go into detail about ethos, because this would take us into practicalities which require more than theoretical arguments about basic aims to decide them. But the theoretical arguments do point us in a certain direction, do help us to see something of what schools should and should not be like, even though more determinate criteria, often arising from features unique to specific schools, will have to be added to these more general ones.

It goes without saying that a school is more likely to achieve its educational aims if its teaching staff agrees about these aims and works together to attain them. This consensus is often lacking in actual schools today, where teachers have often been brought up in very different educational traditions, some holding that all aims should be intrinsic, others putting more stress on career benefits or social service and yet others believing for progressivist or other reasons that any imposition of aims on children is immoral and anti-educational. Schools without this consensus can be superficially well-ordered: there can be *some* common purposes, built round the HCF of the contesting viewpoints; but a danger is that teachers come increasingly to abide by the HCF and bother less and less about linking what they do to more fundamental aims.

Teachers can dovetail their work with their colleagues' to help bring about common purposes only if they have these purposes; and it is desirable for various reasons that these purposes be thought through and agreed at their foundations. Not only do teachers need this rational co-operation properly to achieve their aims: it is also likely to help pupils themselves, especially the older ones, to have a clearer idea of what their schooling is all about if this is reinforced at all points by the whole way in which their school is organised. School organisation can itself be a teacher. It *can*. But it can also be a confuser, an unwitting brainwasher, which leaves pupils bewildered about why they are at school at all.

School organisation must be rationally ordered, but not in *any* way. Consensus might be achieved by pressure from those at the top of power-hierarchies on those below; or democratically, by rational discussion among autonomous moral agents. Teachers are models for children. They teach insensibly by what they are and what they do. If they passively accept what others decree, they may influence children to believe that this is how one should behave. There should be no need to labour the point that this directly contradicts the autonomy aim I have argued they should have. If school organisation is to promote educational aims and not obstruct them, there is only one solution. Teachers must themselves be models of the type of educated person they wish their pupils to become. They, too, must be morally autonomous agents, doing what they do because they think, on reflection, that it is right and not only because someone in authority has told them to do it. The school, like any other place of work, must be a participatory democracy, at least among the staff: if it is not, however its aims approximate to the ideal, its own organisation will get in the way of their realisation (P. White, 1981).

How far this will mean the abolition of present hierarchical structures and in particular the office of headmaster or headmistress would need further discussion. I will add only this. As things are, ironically it is in their schools that children often first learn the importance of status: many a bright 5-year-old is fully *au fait* with the chain of command in her primary school, from the headmaster via the deputy, the head of infants to the class teacher and her part-time auxiliary, after only a week or two in the reception class. Of course, all schools need to be organised efficiently, but there may be other ways of doing it than by reinforcing the tendency which young children easily adopt, of treating authority figures as increasingly god-like the higher they are up the Burnham scale.

It should also go without saying that the ethos of status and submission must be jettisoned also in relations between class teachers and pupils. Authoritarian teaching methods have no place. This is not to say, of course, that teachers should let children do what they like. This would be to reinforce an undesirable belief of another kind – that one's well-being consists in the satisfaction of immediate desire. Teachers are there to fulfil a specific social function, to make children into intelligent, informed and autonomous moral agents. They need not be afraid that to try to get their pupils on the inside of certain forms of knowledge and forms of behaviour is to impose their own subjective values. They are a child's liberators, not his gaolers. But they know, or should know, some of the paths the child must take to reach this freedom; the child does not.

(b) *Curricula*

Let me turn away from ethos, brief though the sketch has been, to a few equally brief remarks about curricula. What kind of curriculum would best be fitted to realise the educational aims I have outlined? We must first distinguish terminal objectives – the achievements expected of pupils at the end of a certain period, say their eleven years of compulsory schooling – from the particular courses they follow in reaching those objectives. The same terminal objectives may be attainable by a variety of routes: an understanding of basic economic concepts, for example, may come via a course in economics neat, via history, current affairs, or a series of projects on local shops and industries. The more one moves from discussing what terminal objectives should be to what particular courses should be like, the less one can lay things down in the abstract, without knowing all sorts of facts about the abilities and interests of specific children, the strengths and weaknesses of the staff available, etc. etc. But it should be possible to say something about terminal objectives without having to look at such details.

As we have seen already, the aims recommended are not compatible with just *any* set of terminal objectives, but place restrictions on what these should be like. If aims can be said to have teeth, these aims have them: they are not so grandiose and all-embracing as to be chargeable with vacuousness. Perhaps their most striking feature is the *breadth* of understanding and of sympathy which they entail. I refer back to the account of the various types of virtue and forms of knowledge required of the educated man, at the beginning of chapter 6.

How far should we rely on school curricula rather than other educative agencies – the ethos of school or of society, the curricula of post-school institutions, the family etc. – to help to bring about these achievements?

It is difficult to say in the abstract, but there are one or two points that should be borne in mind. Let us take it, first of all, that when we talk of 'school curricula' in this context we mean a *compulsory* set of terminal objectives to be achieved via courses of study by the end of the period of compulsory schooling. And what we mean by 'compulsory' objectives here are objectives which are to be insisted on for all children. (Whether it is only the school which does this insisting or another body, e.g. the government, which insists that the school insists is a further question which we can here ignore.) As things are in fact, not all school courses lead to compulsory objectives in this sense. It may also be important for us to ask how far the work of schools should incorporate activities *not* leading to compulsory objectives in this sense – purely voluntary activities, for instance, or activities leading to different objectives for different children. We will come back indeed to these questions a little later on. Meanwhile the focus will be on compulsory terminal objectives for all schoolchildren at the end of their school career. The issue is: how far should we rely on objectives of this sort, rather than other means, to help us reach our educational aims?

One reason why it is difficult to decide the contribution of school curricula in the abstract is that it is not clear how pedagogical labour should be divided between the schools themselves and post-school institutions. Towards the end of chapter 6 I suggested that we might revive the old idea of compulsory part-time education beyond the school-leaving age with officially encouraged voluntary provision beyond the period of part-time study. If we *did* go for something like this, it would be reasonable to determine school terminal objectives by a method of subtraction: one sees what post-school provision can be expected to contribute to total realisation of aims and ensures that schools do work which does not duplicate this. Theoretically it will be easier to do this if we ignore post-school *voluntary* provision and attend only to compulsory courses. We might, for instance – and this is only to be taken as an illustration, not a recommendation – think that a good deal of the knowledge about actual socio-economic arrangements necessary for informed citizenship, might best be acquired in post-school, part-time courses. If we knew that these were compulsory, there would be no reason for insisting on this work being covered at school. Post-school voluntary provision, in adult education, further or higher education, for instance, complicates the picture. If we knew that it was likely that, say, 95 per cent of the population would take advantage of this, we would have a good reason not to insist on their doing at school what they would be doing later. But this presupposes that they know while still schoolchildren that as adults they will be studying art, or science, politics or whatever. Since this condition is unlikely to be met, I propose that we can ignore the contribution of post-school *voluntary* provision in this context.

Since as a matter of empirical fact about the British scene there is no *compulsory* post-school education *either*, we can in present circumstances ignore that, too. In looking at the contribution of educational courses of all types to the realisation of aims *for everyone*, i.e. to creating a society where everyone is an educated man, the only courses which we need bother about are those provided by schools: it is only while pupils are still at school that we can insist on their following educational courses. At the same time all this might cause us to rethink the desirability of part-time continuation education if 16 is too young an age to expect pupils to have reached those educational objectives, to which courses, as distinct from 'ethos', can normally be expected to lead.

To some extent the same principles apply to comparisons of the relative importance of school curricula and ethos. We can apply here, too, the principle of subtraction. If we have reasonable assurance that a certain fraction of the educated man's requirements can be met via the workings of the ethos of the school or the wider social ethos, it seems sensible not to duplicate that area in school curricula, but to let the latter concentrate on what other agencies cannot do. If, for instance, all work-institutions were participatory democracies, then a lot of the educationally necessary work in this area might well be put off until children left school to take a job. In practice, however, as illustrated above, as far as the ethos of society rather than the school is concerned, we often find it working *against* educational aims, in the area not only of democracy but also of consumerism, income-distribution, prevailing moral attitudes, and so on. This suggests a principle not of subtraction, but of *addition*. There is now *more* work for schools (taking their curricula and ethos together) to do, not less: they have not only to work for educational aims directly, as it were: they have also some responsibility to counteract the miseducative work of other institutions and of the general culture.

Given these rather abstract points about school curricula *vis-à-vis* other agencies, is there anything more determinate to say about them? In a longer work there would be innumerable things to say, but here I will restrict myself to one or two brief observations.

First of all, in a society like ours without compulsory post-school provision and where so much in the general social ethos is anti-educational, a large burden falls on schools, not least on their curricula. (I am ignoring, but only for the moment, the contributions which parents can make.) There is a danger that curricula could become seriously overloaded. It makes good sense, therefore, to work out what should go into curricular objectives with some care, so as to ensure that essential ingredients are not left out and that inessentials do not creep in.

All this may sound a bit like the proposals to establish a 'core curriculum' or a 'protected area' of the curriculum, which British governments of both persuasions have been urging since the 'Great Debate' of 1976. In fact, however, the present recommendation is very different from these.

The 'core curriculum' proposal does indeed embody what is said to be 'basic' to every child's education. But its conception of what is 'basic' is a very narrow one. Both major government documents which have incorporated it, the Labour green paper, *Education in Schools* (HMSO, 1977) and the Tory *A Framework for the School Curriculum* (HMSO, 1980), have included a reasonably broad set of educational aims said to be important for all schools, but have played down many of these aims when determining what the 'core' should consist in. The latter boils down in both mainly to English, mathematics, science and a foreign language. (In the 1980 document religious and physical education are also essentials.) No rationale is given in either paper for concentrating on just these things, although it seems pretty clear that this is in line with the many official pronouncements that have been made over the last five or six years about the contribution that schools can make to the revitalising of British industry.

What is 'basic' to a child's education on this view seems to be identified with what is alleged to be basic to industrial needs. But we should be very wary of talk of what is 'basic' in this connection. The term can have different applications and some of them may get tangled together with unfortunate results. In my sketch of the educated man in chapter 6, I spelt out the kinds of dispositions and understanding he requires. It follows from my argument about the important part school curricula must play in our kind of society in realising educational aims that its terminal objectives should be largely built around these. This whole broad range of achievements can be said to be a 'basic' requirement of the educated man. It is 'basic' in that it is a *necessary condition* of educatedness. If a man were brought up without some of these ingredients, without the various moral or prudential virtues, or without a broad understanding of the different possible constituents of the good life, or without an understanding of and disposition towards participatory democracy, if these or other things were lacking, he could not become an educated man. If, on the other hand, he *did* attain these kinds of objectives (and the list is not complete), it would be reasonable to conclude that his teachers could do nothing more to make him educated. The requirements, taken together, would be *sufficient* as well as necessary.

In what way are the 'core' subjects – English, mathematics, science and a foreign language – basic? Are they *necessary* requirements in a child's education? It is not immediately possible to answer this, because the 'core' curriculum consists of *subjects* and not, as we have been understanding things, terminal objectives and sub-objectives thereto. But we can assume that the 'core' idea is translatable into objectives-talk and that the basic requirements are, broadly, literacy, numeracy, an elementary understanding of science especially in its technological applications, and some ability to speak and write a foreign language (since only two years of this is demanded in the core, sights must be set pretty low here).

Now whether the 'core' proposals are industry-oriented or intended as part of a more pupil-centred education, few people will disagree that most of these objectives are worthwhile. Children do need to become literate and numerate and do need an elementary knowledge of science. About foreign languages there is likely to be more dissension. For my own part, I have still failed to discover any good arguments in favour of compulsory languages for all. Although there are many things I would want to change in my book, *Towards a Compulsory Curriculum* (White, 1973), I would still stick by the view I expressed there, that while it is important for reasons to do with a choice of a way of life that pupils come to understand something of what speaking a foreign language involves, that is no reason in itself for them to learn the *skills* of speaking one, not least in the time-consuming way usually found in class-teaching.

Foreign languages apart, however, the 'basic' objectives of the core curriculum are reasonable enough as necessary conditions of anyone's education. Any child deprived of them will suffer an important loss. But to say they are 'basic' in this way does not imply that they are the *only* things that are. The trouble with restricting the 'basics' to so little is that governments may then claim, and with apparent plausibility, that, provided they have raised standards sufficiently in all the four 'core' areas, they have done enough adequately to educate the nation's children. But the claim should be rebutted. It is not enough to provide *some* of the basics: *all* of them are necessary. We need not the 'core' alone, but the whole fruit.

Back to basics? Certainly. School curricula should not be allowed to proliferate in any direction as under our autonomous school system they can do and have done. They have a big burden to carry and the 15,000 hours of compulsory schooling need to be directed more than they usually are towards the fundamentals: *all* the fundamentals.

'And what are these?', I will be asked at this point. 'Seeing that you reject current ideas about "core" curricula, what set of curriculum objectives do you think *should* be laid down for schools to follow? True, you've told us that the sketch of the educated man's achievements at the beginning of chapter 6 should be our starting point. And I can accept your arguments that the school curriculum is only one means among others of helping to bring about the achievements and that we should not assume that all children will have reached the "blurred area" of educatedness by the time they leave school. All right. But as a teacher (or headteacher or education officer or whatever) I need more practicable guidelines than these. Can't you be more specific about your "basics", provide us with detailed proposals about terminal objectives which we can then operationalise, if suitable, into timetabling, staffing and other arrangements?'

It will seem to some a lame defence that this is primarily a book about educational aims in general and only marginally, in this final chapter, about the different ways in which aims may be realised. They may think it lame because they treat an unwillingness or inability to go into details as a sign that the theory is unworkable. I have met this kind of reaction in a different, but related, context. Whenever I talk on the control of the school curriculum, arguing from a philosophical standpoint that its broad outlines should be laid down by the democratic state, I am always pressed to describe the mechanisms by which this could come about. 'What will be the composition of the body which lays down the guidelines?', I am asked. 'What system of monitoring do you envisage, so that the democracy can ensure that schools are doing what they are told?' 'What sanctions would you recommend against the headteacher who refused to toe the line?' When I reply that I am a philosopher of education, not an expert on educational administration, and that I have nothing authoritative to say on these complex matters, there is always a deputy head in the back row who turns at that point to her neighbour with a knowing smile. From this and from other evident signs of exasperation elsewhere in the audience, I know I am done for. But is their attitude reasonable? Why must the proponent of a practical theory – e.g. about who should determine curricula or about what the aims of education should be – be able to say in detail how his proposals might be realised? To take a parallel case, I don't know, as a matter of fact, who dreamed up the idea of a 'green belt' around London and other major cities. Most people will agree that the idea was sound in principle: it set limits to urban sprawl. But it would have been hard on its originator if his idea had been brushed aside at the outset on the grounds that he had not thought through what action should be taken against transgressors, for example, or what new staff local authorities would need to employ in order to implement it. These questions do indeed require answers if the idea is ever to be put into effect. But there is no onus on its originator to produce them. The most he needs to argue is that his idea is not unrealisable in principle: he can leave it to the administrative ingenuity of others, if he so wishes, to work out ways and means. If, of course, his critics can show that there is something so radically impractical about his scheme that it is not worth entertaining, that is quite another matter.

To apply this last point to the school curriculum. I do not think it is likely that critics will find my proposed aims obviously unrealisable: it is not as though I were urging, for instance, that children leaving infant school know all about calculus. If people do so object, however, the onus is in any case on them to say what is wrong. But the more probable charge will be, as I have said, that I fail to deliver the goods at the more practical level where they are needed. I can only reply that it was never my intention to do so. First things first.

In any case, it would not be at all easy to spell out a viable set of curriculum objectives in line with my general theory. All kinds of particular judgments would be called for, many of which would involve trade-offs between conflicting considerations. How far, for instance, would guidelines on the physical sciences emphasise intrinsic values, instrumental-prudential or instrumental-moral/political benefits? What I have said in this book gives *some* indications of priorities, but *judgment* is still unavoidable. The same is true about how educational labour should be divided between school curricula on the one hand and other agencies (school ethos, post-school education, social institutions etc.) on the other. These are all complex matters, almost certainly beyond the powers of any single individual, as contrasted with, say, a National Educational Board, to resolve. There is no one right set of answers – just as there is no one right way of implementing green-belt legislation. There is, above all, no timeless, eternally valid school curriculum. As society in general changes – as more, or less, of the task of educating is undertaken by institutions other than the school – so the role and content of the curriculum should shrink or expand. To point out these complexities may be salutary in itself. Too often teachers expect 'curriculum theorists', working as individuals, to come up with practicable guidelines; too often the theorists themselves – I do not exonerate myself – have been ready to answer the call. The same, given our British autonomous school system, applies to headteachers. To see the content of the curriculum as too complex an issue to be left to individuals is to take a step forward. As for the composition of any National Educational Board or other body to whom such problems were remitted, I hope you will now bear with me when I say, 'But that's another question!'

One thing which it would be reasonable to ask any such Board or other body to do would be to plan the eleven years of compulsory schooling which we have now as a unified whole. I know I am on safe ground in claiming that in English schools this unified planning *never* occurs. This may come as a shock to people outside the education service. It seems so logical, so rational to make the broad outlines of what children of 6 and 9 do cohere with later expectations of them at 13 or 16, that it is hard to see how any national education service could avoid doing this. Elsewhere in the world most do this, in fact. But not the English. In this country the tradition – at least since 1926 – has been for each school to be responsible for its own curricular objectives and arrangements. (For the changes in 1926, see White, 1975.) Each primary school is autonomous; so is each secondary school fed by that primary school. Both areas plan their curricula independently of each other. Even within schools there is by no means always curricular continuity from one year-group to the next; in primary schools, indeed, the custom has been to leave each class teacher very wide powers to decide on what curriculum he or she considers most suitable.

One effect of curricular autonomy both between schools and within them is that the total package which any particular child receives is almost bound to be inadequate in some way. Work gets repeated in different years; important gaps appear; pupils find it difficult to cotton on to new topics because they lack the prerequisite understanding, and so on.

I do not want to overstate the case. There is plenty of evidence of solid curricular success. But it is hard to deny that things could be improved if curricula were planned on an eleven-year basis. This might well mean that the foundations of learning in such areas as science, history, the arts and social studies could be laid far earlier than they often are today. Understanding is a matter of degree, not an all-or-nothing affair. Children of 8 or 9 may not be capable of a very profound understanding of such concepts as democracy, or the trade balance, or electricity, but there is no reason why they should not have *some* grasp of these things, as well as some purchase on recent world history and current affairs and some capacity to enjoy music, poetry and the other arts. Of these areas, the arts seem to come off best in practice (leaving aside the question whether schools spend too long on getting children to produce their own art at the expense of acquainting them with others'). But in an eleven-year plan, where the basics are all-important and there is a strong case for arranging things as economically as possible, *every* subject area would do well to lay its foundations early, rather than treating concepts like democracy and the others as suitable only for secondary children of a certain maturity. That way all sorts of vital concepts and topics are left until the last two or three years of the eleven-year programme, when there is often insufficient time to deal with them properly. The consequence is that the first eight or nine years of that period are often rather thin in educational content. There is a well-known but very regrettable syndrome in English schools. I perhaps overstated just now the degree of curricular independence and discontinuity there is between different parts of the system, for there *is* a kind of consensus among teachers about who should teach what when. It falls very far short of the integrated eleven-year programme I have been calling for, and takes a rather peculiar negative or defensive form. Infant teachers are often wary of encroaching on the curricular territory of the junior school and restrict their terminal objectives accordingly. Junior teachers often think it no business of theirs to give structured courses in history, geography or science since work of this kind – as distinct from isolated topic work – belongs in their view to the secondary school. Secondary teachers themselves tend to reinforce this presumption: 'as long as the children come up to us keen and eager to learn, that's all that matters'; 'it is only in the secondary school that the "real" work of education begins.'

The effect of all this after-you-Clauding is to slow down the pace at which children work in the first eight or nine years, leaving too much to the last two or three, when, as things are, public examinations begin to fill the horizon. There are other pressures at work in the same direction. Educational psychology is still dominated by Piagetian theory, which is often taken to imply that it is no use doing anything very intellectually demanding with children of primary age, since they are only at the stage of 'concrete operations' and would not understand. Recent philosophical and psychological critiques of Piaget should help to dispel this misconception: children's minds do not develop naturally and in due season like biological entities; conceptual schemes are acquired only in social interaction and can be extended by deliberate intervention.[1] Another cause of this same tendency to slow the pace at which children learn is the interest which capitalist institutions have long had in obstructing the formation of too knowledgeable a work-force. In eleven years of schooling children *could* learn a very great deal, a very great deal, moreover, which could open their eyes to socio-economic reality and make them unwilling to knuckle down to the submissive and often mindless regime which modern industry requires of them.

An end, therefore, to spreading learning thinly over the years! It is time in this matter as in many others to put our conventional reactions into reverse, to pack things more tightly into the earlier years. This is not at all to be confused with the philosophy of those parents who move their children out of state into private schools so that they can be fully occupied with Latin, clause-analysis and extra maths throughout the day and halfway through the evening. My sketch of the educated man should show I hold no brief for such silly academicism. But people, these parents included, do often rightly worry that children could be stretched more than they are. Inspectors' reports justify their apprehensions. An eleven-year programme on the lines suggested could do much to allay them.

I must still do more to make it quite plain that I don't want to turn young children into learning machines or to force concepts and information into them which are quite inappropriate. My view is that if the 15,000 hours of compulsory schooling were more carefully thought through, there would be *plenty* of time to do all the things I have been pressing for for younger children. I see no reason, indeed, why the amount of compulsory schooling each child receives each day should not be significantly *reduced*, thus allowing him much more time to spend, if he so wills it, on purely voluntary activities. I continue to be attracted by the idea I floated in *Towards a Compulsory Curriculum* that we might think of introducing a properly planned system of voluntary learning, either on school premises or in purpose-built institutions, where children can do anything from extra gymnastics, maths or painting to learning to play an instrument, doing woodwork or making radios. The compulsory part of the school day could be kept for the basics (in my enlarged sense), thus trying to ensure that no child lost the chance of becoming an educated person. In the voluntary part children could do what lies over and above, or outside, this basic area.

This sort of division would do something to resolve the tension between supporters of common-curricular provision for all children and those who think schooling should be tailored more to differing needs and interests. If the arguments presented here for the 'basics' are valid, they are valid, *prima facie*, for all children. Unless good reasons are available to the contrary, the compulsory eleven-year curriculum should be common to all. In some cases, good reasons *can* be given: the worst cases of mental subnormality will be incapable of virtually all of it, and children with a particular affliction like blindness or deafness may be incapable of some of it. I have already argued against reserving a broad-ranging education of this sort to an elite and need not repeat earlier points.

While common needs could thus be catered for in the compulsory part of the school day, there would be plenty of opportunity in the voluntary part for children to diverge along paths of their own choice. Quicker children, for instance, would be able to take up all sorts of things in further depth (see above). The innovation would not only be in line with the general principle of liberty, whereby no one should be compelled into any course of action beyond a certain point, i.e. where there are no longer good overriding reasons to constrain him; it would also fit hand in glove with the ideal of personal autonomy, since children would be encouraged from an early age to make up their own minds how best to use the non-compulsory time now given them.

Should the common compulsory curriculum last for the whole eleven years, i.e. up to 16? Or should pupils be allowed to specialise before that point? Again, the new dual system would seem to fit the bill. The intellectual and dispositional requirements of the educated man need not be set enormously high. There is no reason to insist on the very high level of intellectual attainment that the highest-flying of our secondary schools set themselves, for instance. We are interested in creating an informed community of morally autonomous co-operative individuals, not in pushing children over bigger and bigger hurdles *en route* to bigger and bigger pay packets or other delicacies. But even though our hurdles will not be high, there will still be plenty to learn over the eleven-year period, especially towards the end of it when the whole complex structure of what the pupil learns assumes its final shape and its vital keystones are put in position. The last years of compulsory education will have increasingly to be committed to the difficult and time-consuming tasks of integrating all the separate elements of one's learning into a unified plan of life – not a final blueprint, to be sure, but a first, if inadequate, sketch. It is not before this time that pupils may be expected to see, as they *must* see if they are to be autonomous beings, the underlying principles and goals of their own education. Some may need longer. I have already hinted at the probable desirability of compulsory continuation education beyond 16. Some, but surely very few, will need less time for these integrating tasks. Perhaps they should be allowed to leave school before 16. But the majority will be likely to need all their eleven years on some kind of compulsory course.

There is no reason, however, why the proportion of time spent on compulsory rather than voluntary activities should always remain constant. The autonomy ideal would be compatible, other things being equal, with a progressive enlargement of the voluntary area, so that opportunities for following one's particular enthusiasms were maximised. This is not quite the same as recommending that the common area of the curriculum shrinks in favour of 'specialisation' in the later years of schooling, at least as this term is normally understood. For 'specialised' courses are still usually compulsory for the child (i.e. she cannot not do them), while voluntary activities are free to be taken up or not as she wishes. It is in this voluntary part of the school day that personal commitment and enthusiasm can be given full rein. This is not at all to say that compulsory studies should lack these qualities. 'Compulsion' in this context does not mean forcing children to learn against their will. The process of education is a progressive shaping of the nature-given desires discussed in Chapter 3 (above p. 49), whereby, for instance, innate curiosity becomes channelled into a love of history or science. Teachers of compulsory curricular activities have every reason to work with nature in this way, to try to generate such enthusiasm for their subject (etc.) that their pupils would want to engage in it even if it were not compulsory. But at the same time it is only realistic to admit that not all children will be passionately committed to all aspects of their compulsory curriculum all the time. It would be odd if they were. Commitment tends to channel itself in particular directions. Of course, the teacher of compulsory activities must go on trying to keep interest alive and rekindle it when it dies, but sometimes this is bound to be an uphill task, at least with some pupils. A voluntary system offers an area of pure spontaneity where that vital continuity with our nature-given selves can be promoted.

I said just above that *other things being equal* there was a case for a progressive enlargement of the voluntary area at the expense of the compulsory. Whether other things *were* equal would depend, for instance, on such things as how much of the 'basics' could be covered in earlier years and how much would have to be left until later; and how time-consuming the integrative tasks just mentioned would prove to be in practice.

Except for one brief remark I will leave my comments on the content and organisation of the school curriculum at that point. The whole topic is a large one and would need a treatise to itself. But I must say a word about examinations. I have already mentioned the bad effects of O and A level and CSE. I see no reason why pupils following this sort of curriculum should be tested by public examinations. Records of their progress would show just as well how well they had done. Or even better: for they could be more detailed and could comment on qualities of character unassessable by written papers.[2] Secondary schools with public examinations can get by only too easily without thinking through their aims: examination success provides them with an aim ready-made – but at the cost of some pupils' seeing curriculum content largely as a means of gaining a certificate, so that it matters little whether they do Latin or extra maths or British Constitution, as long as this gives them an extra O level or increases their chance of a B or C at A level and consequently of a university place.

With this all-too-brief comment I conclude my remarks about the content of the curriculum. At least I hope it should be evident by now where I think the responsibility for determining school curricula should lie. It cannot be left, as has recently been the norm in Britain, to head teachers and their staffs. What the content of the curriculum should be cannot be divorced from what the aims of education should be; and this in its turn is inextricable, or should be inextricable, from still wider considerations about the well-being of the community. That is why decisions at least about the broad framework of the curriculum are unavoidably political decisions. Since they are, there is every reason to take the power to make them out of the hands of a particular section of the community: head teachers and their staffs are no more professionally equipped than doctors or train drivers to decide how society as a whole should develop. In some way, curricular decisions must be brought under the democratic control of the community. The points raised just above, that what should go into school curricula should not be decided without on the one hand assessing the likely educative influence of the ethos of school and society, and on the other seeing what post-school education can contribute, reinforce the ill-advisedness of leaving curricular decisions to the schools themselves: wider perspectives are necessary than those likely to be available to heads and their staffs. None of this argument against the school's autonomy is meant to show that teachers should have no responsibilities in the curricular field. The argument has been about the broad framework of the curriculum only. Over many details teachers often *do* have a professional expertise that other persons lack. Curriculum content has to be married to the particular capabilities and interests of particular children. Only teachers are in a position to know these capabilities and interests and hence how best to shape the content to fit them. They must be given maximum flexibility to interpret any democratically decided guidelines according to their own professional judgment: the familiar continental system of prescribing in detail the routes to terminal objectives as well as the objectives themselves has very little to recommend it. Note, too, that it is *classroom teachers* who are to have the power to determine these details. Between classroom teachers on the one side and democratic decision-makers on the other, there are no further curricular powers to be left to the special province of head teachers. This, as well as their probably harmful effect on children's attitudes towards status and democratic development, is one more good reason for abolishing or radically modifying their role.

(3)   *Other educational institutions*
I turn, briefly, to the role that three other sorts of educational institution can play in realising aims: (a) post-school institutions (b) teacher education institutions (c) the family.

(a)   *Post-school institutions*
Many will not reach the blurred boundaries of educatedness by the age of 16. Most, perhaps. I have already suggested that we might consider reviving the idea of compulsory part-time continuation education for this purpose. There is no need to go over these points again.

It would not be appropriate to look into the sorts of post-school teaching institutions necessary for other aims than the ones I am concerned with, e.g. with training for specific jobs or ranges of jobs, or with recreational courses. These are important topics but they fall outside my remit.

But I would like to comment on the educative role of *universities*, since this links up with more general themes in this book. It is often taken as read that universities are educational institutions. People – some people – 'finish their education' at universities: the latter continue and bring to fruition the work done in schools. At least, so it is said. But it is very important to remember that this sort of thing is usually said against the background of a certain view of education, the view, namely, that education is to do with the possession or pursuit of learning for its own sake. If this is already given as the aim of education, and if it is also given that education should seek to develop pupil's capacities to the full, there seems to be no need to provide a further justification for the existence of universities. They are simply helping society to achieve this aim more nearly, by producing people – those people with the highest capacities – with a higher level of educatedness. Of course, there may be practical questions raised about the justifiability of universities when public money spent on them might go elsewhere: if there are only enough university places for a few, what priority has the high-level education of a small minority among competing social ends? But a society with a rapidly growing economy may well divert some of its wealth to increasing the number of university places (or, more generally, places in higher education) with the ultimate aim of enabling everyone capable of higher education to benefit from it. Our own society adopted this point of view in the 1960s, following the report of the Robbins Committee in 1963.

I have serious misgivings about all this. I have already argued against the theory that education should seek to develop capacities to the full (see pp. 35–7). And if, as I have also argued in chapter 2, the aim of education is not to be 'knowledge for its own sake', but something more like what has been proposed in this book, it is no longer at all obvious that universities are always educational institutions. To be so, they would have to help students to form an integrated life-plan worked out from a moral point of view. Some moves to broaden the content of university courses may have something like this in mind; and specialised courses sometimes interpret their specialism so broadly that it can come to fulfil this role: this may be true of some departments of literature or of philosophy, for instance. But very often universities see their teaching function not in this way at all, but as concerned with the specialised pursuit of knowledge for its own sake. (I omit their interest in applied knowledge. This brings in aims, like training for a particular profession, like engineering, medicine or the law, which are not usually seen as *educational* aims, certainly not by the 'knowledge-for-its-own-sake' school. I also omit their role as institutions of research and scholarship.)

In so far as universities move away from specialisation towards the tasks of person integration, they will be doing the same kind of job as the continuation schools mentioned earlier. For this reason, there is no need, perhaps, for two different kinds of institution. We can keep something of the spirit of Robbins, agreeing that, as resources allow, more and more people should be allowed to pursue their education at a higher level, as long as we change the concept of education on the lines suggested.

(b)   *Teacher education institutions*

A reassessment of educational aims on the lines suggested carries implications, too, for colleges and departments of teacher education. The chief one is that teachers should be discouraged from seeing their work as self-contained, disconnected from the wider interests of the community. A teacher should not be, among other things, a high priest of culture, inspiring others to worship at the altar of knowledge for its own sake. By this I do *not* mean that gifted teachers of literature, pure mathematics or whatever should be chased out of their schools, only that they should ideally be aware how their subjects fit into the larger pattern of individual and community well-being, and transmit something of this awareness to their pupils. Neither should the teacher be, secondly, the teacher-psychologist I criticised in chapter 3, the supposed scientific authority on the nature of the child and the laws of his development. Psychological studies may well have some place in the education of teachers, but they should not have the central place which they had in the days of child-centred dominance. Both these inward-looking conceptions of the teacher must go. Whatever his particular subject or expertise, the teacher should be able to connect it to larger purposes. He will need a broadly philosophical understanding of many of the fundamental problems of human well-being and life in a community discussed in this book; and he will need a sound knowledge of the main features of his own society in their historical, sociological and economic perspectives. As to how he should acquire this knowledge, I hold no particular brief for pre-service training, where more immediate problems of classroom control and pupil-stimulation tend to leave little time for the more extended reflection required. *Something*, no doubt, could and should be done in this direction during initial training, but most will have to be left to in-service education. I stated earlier my belief that serving teachers need more time for reflection about what they are doing. It is anti-educational to pin them to specific teaching duties, inside or outside the classroom, for virtually all their working week, as so often happens now. The result is often only the lifeless, mechanical regime with which all of us are in different contexts familiar. If teachers were given more time for reflection — stimulated not only by formal in-service classes, but also, and perhaps more importantly, by discussion with their colleagues — not only would the tiny details of their classroom work be imbued with a new and wider meaning, but the work of the school as a whole would rest far more than it typically does today on a foundation of shared understanding, of attitudes and beliefs held in common. Those who teach, for instance, in today's comprehensive schools know how often their work is vitiated by ideological gulfs among the staff. Again, I must make it plain that I am *not* proposing that members of a staff should think alike on every particular. Controversy, dispute, independence of mind are highly desirable. But if any institution is to work efficiently, its members must share certain beliefs and commitments. All I am asking for is an *extension* of this common background which teachers can assume each other to possess. Teachers ought to agree to a very large extent about their fundamental aims. If they do, this agreement will get built into the ethos of the school and thus an awareness of these larger purposes will be insensibly transmitted to the pupils themselves. It would be far from 'selfish' on the part of teachers to demand more time for reflection at the expense of classroom duties. Their pupils would be the first to benefit.

(c) *The family*

It is a truism, but a truism often overlooked, that by the time a child arrives at school at the age of 5, the basic structures of his later intellectual and moral achievements have been built into his mind. Parents have enormous opportunities, although many of them seem not fully to recognise this, to help form these basic structures. The opportunities begin virtually at birth and are greatly enlarged as the child's understanding of language develops. Parents are the child's first educators. Their achievements in the early years should dovetail with the work of nursery and infant teachers later on. It would seem to follow, for much the same reasons as in the last paragraph, that the work of both parent and teacher should be guided by common assumptions about education and its aims: radical divergence of outlook may well leave the child whom they are both educating confused and unable to learn. Parents, too, therefore, have as much need as teachers to reflect about the larger aims of education. This is not an *option*, which some especially educationally attuned parents may take up if they want to. It is more an obligation: parents have a duty to lay the proper foundations of their child's education, and so have a duty to think out what this education should basically be about.

This line of thought ends in a conclusion which far from supports the *status quo*. Today the talk is all of parents' rights – their right to choose where their child shall be educated, their rights over the curriculum, their right to have their child brought up in their own religion. But what is the basis of such rights? From the empirical fact that one has brought a child into the world, one can draw no ethical conclusion about what one should do or has the moral right to do. True, parents may have *legal* rights over their children of various kinds, but we are concerned here with a moral and not a legal issue. If biology is not a basis for moral rights, what is? The only rights to which a parent *qua* parent seems to me entitled derive from his responsibilities in bringing up a child. It is because parents are normally entrusted with these responsibilities that they have the right, for instance, to prevent anyone who wishes to from sharing them unless he is authorised, e.g. as a teacher, to do so: one empirical assumption underlying this is that children's development will be hindered by such radical discontinuities in upbringing. Parental rights derive, therefore, from parental obligations. They do not stand on their own.

If this is correct, a problem immediately arises about the parent's alleged right to bring a child up in his own religion, political persuasion or *weltanschauung*. If the parent has an obligation to bring up his child as a morally autonomous person, he cannot at the same time have the right to indoctrinate him with any beliefs whatsoever, since some beliefs may contradict those on which his educational endeavours should be based. It is hard to see, for instance, how a desire for one's child's moral autonomy is compatible with the attempt to make him into a good Christian, Muslim or orthodox Jew. It is equally hard to see how the wish that he become a co-operative member of a democratic community squares with wanting him to have an 'exclusive', e.g. public school, education, designed to make him a cut above the rest. The unavoidable implication seems to be that parents should not be left with this freedom to indoctrinate. Ways must be found, by compulsion, persuasion or enlightened public opinion, to prevent them from hindering the proper education of their children. I am aware that this suggestion will be far from universally welcomed. The freedom of the parent to bring up his own children according to his own lights has long seemed sacrosanct. But I would urge objectors to reflect on the rational basis of this belief. *Has* it a rational basis, in fact? Or is it prejudice?

Parents, in short, have obligations as educators, not independent rights as progenitors. School teachers also have obligations as educators. In their case we require courses of training, professional qualifications. Are parents in any relevantly different position? Should the community insist in some way that parents be intellectually equipped to carry out their obligations? It would seem to follow logically from the thesis, although I am not clear how in practice it could be realised. Of course, once the community was already moving in the direction I have indicated, the problem would to some extent look after itself. In the limiting, ideal, case, everybody would be brought up as an informed, morally autonomous person. When he became a parent, he would know from his own experience to what ends his child's upbringing should be directed. True, this would not equip him with an understanding of the detailed routes he might follow on the way to these ends, and the community might still need to be assured that he acquires this understanding. For the moment, as with other things, we must rely less, perhaps, than we can in the future on the workings of a beneficent social ethos and more on more formal requirements.

A utopian theory?

This concludes all I have space for here on the realisation of education's aims. It also concludes the argument of the book as a whole.

One probable reaction to this larger argument in certain quarters will be that it is 'utopian'. I state that on inductive grounds: many of the things I have written in the past have elicited just this response and I do not see why the present book should be an exception.

To label a thesis 'utopian' is usually to condemn it in some way, but not always in the same way. One thing an objector might want to say of the present scheme is that it presents a picture of a perfect society which is quite unrealisable. John Passmore has recently reminded us in his

Perfectibility of Man of all the varied accounts which have been given through the ages of a golden age, sometimes in the past, sometimes in the future, sometimes out of time altogether (Passmore, 1970). Do not my frequent references to an outward-looking participatory democracy of morally autonomous men constitute just another of these dream-pictures?

I would not like to think so. I *don't* believe in a golden age, and I agree with Passmore about the totalitarian tendencies often associated with such a belief. Man is not perfectible: he will always have faults and shortcomings and so, therefore, will any community in which he lives. I offer my suggestions about educational aims not with an eye on Eldorado but in a far more practical spirit. No one will deny that our present thinking about the aims of education in our society, not least within the education system itself, is in a mess: we are nowhere near agreeing collectively on where we should be going. I hope at the least that I've made the central issues a little clearer; and at the most, perhaps, that I've indicated one possible way forward. All I would stick by is that it is forward from where we are now. Where it might lead to *in the end* is not something that interests me particularly. It will not, at any rate, be Perfection.

A second charge of 'utopianism' might be that, whether or not I believe in perfectibility, I am laying down a *blueprint* for a society and for an education system. Like the many writers on this topic who are tempted in this direction, I fail to realise that a society must change constantly if it is not to ossify. 'Piecemeal social engineering', as Karl Popper put it, is what is needed, not 'utopian' planning.

I must admit that I am less averse to blueprints than I am to perfectibility. There is nothing intrinsically amiss with a scheme of improvement. But I would rebut the charge that the kind of blueprint I have put forward is likely to confine a society, to rigidify it in the way alleged. It is a higher order blueprint, designed to prevent the hegemony of more determinate blueprints enshrining particular concepts of the good life.

Some people, finally, might label the thesis 'utopian' because it cannot be realised in foreseeable social conditions. It demands, for instance, a democratisation of industry. But this in turn might be taken to entail that the ownership of industrial firms passes from the shareholders to those in democratic control, i.e. nothing short of the end of the capitalist system. Even if this is desirable, it is hardly likely to come about for, say, another half-century or so. It may be true that teachers in schools are casting about for a viable set of aims; but as remote a set as this is not likely to cut much ice. Again, there's not much point in giving everyone as rich an education as this if the amount of work the community requires to sustain itself leaves him insufficient time or energy to shape such a personal response. Perhaps in a century or so this may be possible; but what can educators aim at in the interim?

But can one peer into the future in this way and see what can't be done? The incidence of revolutionary change in our own century, both politically and technologically, should make us think carefully before putting up objections of this kind. In any case the objection overlooks the contribution which an education of the sort proposed could make in speeding up such achievements. A population *au fait* with the rationale of a participatory democracy is less likely to tolerate an autocratic or oligarchic organisation of industry than a population, like today's, which has never received a political education; and a society which has once come to see the distinction between mere *labour*, on the one hand, and some kind of *work* which is an expression of one's deepest reflections about human life, is likely to do more to tilt the scales from the former to the latter than an unenlightened society for whom labour is contrasted only with relaxation or pleasure. (I do not wish to imply that the scales can be tilted all the way. Uninteresting or unpleasant work will perhaps always be with us, perhaps on a large scale. But it can in principle be more equitably shared, so that we all have more time for activities of a more fulfilling sort – for 'work' as I have put it.) Again, are we really so desperately far from the possibilities in question? Industrial democracy of some sort is already practised in places and may be on the British statute book before long. Capitalism is in crisis: no one knows how quickly its undemocratic features can be eliminated. The working week is short enough in some industries already to allow a fuller participation in a more reflective form of life. Increasingly, people are lacking not so much in time but in ideas how best to fill it.

I do not believe, in short, that the society projected in this book is 'utopian' in the sense of being unrealisable in foreseeable socio-economic conditions. If it is otherwise acceptable, the issue of its realisability is eminently worth putting to the test.

Notes

Preface

1   The nearest attempt has been in Downie *et al.* (1974), chs 3, 4.
2   Examples (among many) of recent philosophical involvement in practical affairs are to be found in Glover, J., *Causing Death and Saving Lives* (Penguin, 1977); Singer, P., *Practical Ethics* (Cambridge, 1979); and in the journal *Philosophy and Public Affairs* (1972 to date).

2   Intrinsic aims

1   For a fuller discussion of Cooper's arguments for selective education in Cooper (1980), see White, P. and White, J., 'David Cooper's Illusions' in *Journal of Philosophy of Education*, vol. 14, no. 2, 1980.

3   The good of the pupil

1   For further discussion of psychological hedonism (the theory that we only ever act for the sake of pleasure), see Brandt, R. B., *Ethical Theory* (Prentice-Hall, 1959), pp. 307–14; Gosling, J. C. B., *Pleasure and Desire* (Oxford, 1969).
2   I am indebted to Susan Wolfson for this point.
3   The gist of the following objections comes from my colleague, Ray Elliott, to whom I am very grateful. In expressing the second objection, I was also influenced by D. Ieuan Lloyd's article 'The Rational Curriculum: a Critique', *Journal of Curriculum Studies*, vol. 12, no. 4, 1980, in which he made some telling criticisms of my earlier book *Towards a Compulsory Curriculum*.
4   Keith Thompson pressed me hard on such problems of categorisation in Thompson, K. and White, J., *Curriculum Development: a Dialogue* (Pitman, 1975), Section 2.

4 The good of society (1): economic, moral and pupil-centred aims

1 Schools who 'tread the path of compromise' do not always do this as a deliberate, agreed policy. Sometimes internal differences of opinion happen to generate this outcome.

2 See Williams, B., 'Egoism and Altruism' in *Problems of the Self* (Cambridge, 1973).

3 I am using 'moral development' here to cover moral learning of all kinds and not in the sense in which 'development' is sometimes *contrasted* with 'learning'.

4 There are complications here, to do with the justice or injustice of 'reverse discrimination'. See Dworkin, R., 'Reverse Discrimination' in his *Taking Rights Seriously* (Duckworth, 1977) and Nagel, T., 'The Policy of Preference' in his *Mortal Questions* (Cambridge, 1979).

5 See Mackie, J. L. (1977). His book argues for a morality of limited altruism, centring around one's own concerns and those of those near to one. I am not imputing to it, however, all the features of what I have called 'minimalist morality'.

5 The good of society (2): moral aims in their economic and political aspects

1 The most striking evidence comes from the Mondragon co-operatives of the Spanish Basque country. Beginning from scratch in 1956, by 1976 this group of producer co-operatives comprised sixty-two industrial enterprises (including high-technology ones, e.g. producing machine-tools) and 15,000 workers. It has continued to expand since that date. It has its own bank, which finances new co-operatives, as well as its own technical college, schools, housing schemes, consumer stores etc. This is a fast-growing participatory democracy whose future progress will be followed with great interest. See Oakeshott R., *The Case for Workers' Co-ops* (Routledge & Kegan Paul, 1978), ch. 10.

Mondragon is not, of course, a large-scale political democracy at national level. As for the claim that the 'common man' is intellectually incapable of helping to run a democracy of this latter type, part of the answer is that, as stated in the text, this kind of democracy must be based on and grow out of participatory democracy on a smaller scale, e.g. in work-places. This is why evidence drawn from an expanding co-operative group like Mondragon is important.

In addition, one should not assume that the common man will need to know about *every* facet of political arrangements. Some things will need to be understood by everybody; in more specific areas different people can build up different bodies of expertise. See note 2 below.

2   See White, P. A., 'Education, Democracy and the Public Interest' in Peters, R. S. (ed.), *The Philosophy of Education* (Oxford, 1973), and her 'Political education in a democracy: the implications for teacher education' *Journal of Further and Higher Education*, vol. 1, no. 3.

3   Not the factory-made white sliced loaves I referred to earlier.

4   For further discussion of this issue, see Benn, S., 'The Problematic Rationality of Political Participation' in Laslett, P. and Fishkin, J. (eds), *Philosophy, Politics and Society* (Fifth Series) (Blackwell, 1979).

7   The realisation of aims

1   For philosophical criticisms of Piaget see Hamlyn, D. W., *Experience and the Growth of Understanding* (Routledge & Kegan Paul, 1978), ch. 4. For psychological criticisms, see Donaldson, M., *Children's Minds* (Fontana, 1978).

2   For a recent philosophical discussion of assessment, see Dearden, R. F., 'The Assessment of Learning' in *British Journal of Educational Studies*, vol. 27, no. 2, June 1979.

Bibliography

A Her Majesty's Stationery Office (DES) Publications
    Education in Schools (1977)
    Primary Education in England (1978)
    Special Educational Needs (1978) ('The Warnock Report')
    A Framework for the School Curriculum (1980)

B Books and articles

ASHTON, P., KEEN, P., DAVIES, F. and HOLLEY, B. J. (1975), *The Aims of Primary Education: A Study of Teachers' Opinions*, Macmillan.

BUTLER, J. (1726), *Fifteen Sermons*.

COOPER, D. E. (1980), *Illusions of Equality*, Routledge & Kegan Paul.

DEARDEN, R. F. (1968), *Philosophy of Primary Education*, Routledge & Kegan Paul.

DEWEY, J. (1916), *Democracy and Education*, Macmillan, New York.

DOWNIE, R., LOUDFOOT, E. and TELFER, E. (1974), *Education and Personal Relationships: A Philosophical Study*, Methuen.

EDGLEY, R. (1980), 'Education, Work and Politics', *Journal of Philosophy of Education*, vol. 14, no. 1, 1980.

GORDON, P. and WHITE, J. (1979), *Philosophers as Educational Reformers*, Routledge & Kegan Paul.

GREEN, T. H. (1883), *Prolegomena to Ethics*, A. C. Bradley (ed.), Clarendon Press, Oxford. Reprinted Apollo Edition, 1969.

HABERMAS, J. (1976), *Legitimation Crisis*, Heinemann.

HARGREAVES, D. H. (1980), 'A Sociological Critique of Individualism in Education', *British Journal of Educational Studies*, vol. 28, no. 3, October 1980.

HIRST, P. H. (1965), 'Liberal Education and the Nature of Knowledge' in Archambault, R. D. (ed.), *Philosophical Analysis and Education*, Routledge & Kegan Paul.

MABBOTT, J. D. (1948), *The State and the Citizen*, Hutchinson.

MACINTYRE, A. (1964), 'Against Utilitarianism', in Hollins, T. H. B. (ed.), *Aims in Education*, Manchester University Press.

MACKIE, J. L. (1977), *Ethics: Inventing Right and Wrong*, Penguin.

MIDGLEY, M. (1979), *Beast and Man*, Harvester.

MILL, J. S. (1859), 'On Liberty' in *Utilitarianism, Liberty and Representative Government*, Everyman's.

NUNN, T. P. (1920), *Education, its data and first principles*, Arnold.

PASSMORE, J. A. (1970), *The Perfectibility of Man*, Duckworth.

PETERS, R. S. (1959), 'Must an Educator Have an Aim?' in *Authority, Responsibility and Education*, Allen & Unwin.

PETERS, R. S. (1966), *Ethics and Education*, Allen & Unwin.

RAWLS, J. (1971), *A Theory of Justice*, Oxford University Press.

SINGER, P. (1979), 'Famine, Affluence and Morality', in Laslett, J. and Fishkin, J. (eds), *Philosophy, Politics and Society* (fifth series).

STRADLING, R. (1977), *The Political Awareness of the School Leaver*, Hansard Society, Blackwell.

TAWNEY, R. H. (1926), *Religion and the Rise of Capitalism*, Penguin, 1938.

WHITE, J. (1973), *Towards a Compulsory Curriculum*, Routledge & Kegan Paul.

WHITE, J. (1974), 'Intelligence and the Logic of the Nature-Nurture Issue', *Proceedings of the Philosophy of Education Society*, vol. 8, no. 1, January 1974.

WHITE, J. (1975), 'The End of the Compulsory Curriculum' in *The Curriculum: The Doris Lee Lectures, Studies in Education 2*, University of London Institute of Education.

WHITE, J. see also GORDON, P.

WHITE, P. (1979), 'Work-Place Democracy and Political Education', *Journal of Philosophy of Education*, vol. 13, 1979.

WHITE, P. (1981), 'Political Education and School Organisation, or How to Run a School and Educate People at the Same Time', in Fisk, D. *et al.* (eds), *Issues for the Eighties: Some Central Questions of Education*, Batsford.

WHITEHEAD, A. N. (1929), *The Aims of Education*, Williams & Norgate.

Index

Ability, 136–8; ceilings of, 20–1, 35–7, 117–18, 137; and income, 142–3; *see also* Children

Academic disciplines, 20

Adult education, *see* Education, adult

Altruism, 67, 80, 85–90, 99, 100, 102, 107

Amoralism, 68, 128–9; *see also* Egoism

Arbitrariness, 30, 34–5, 37, 81, 83, 97, 107

'Aristotelian principle', the, 47

Aristotle, 12, 18, 22, 117

Art, 2, 14, 18, 44–6, 54–5, 63–5, 102, 133, 157

Ashton, P., *et al.*, 24, 63

Autonomy: intellectual, 127; moral, 92–107, 110, 120, 140, 143–4, 148–9; personal, 2, 25–6, 39–41, 50–1, 62, 67, 70–1, 92, 98, 121, 123, 126, 128, 133, 142–3, 159–60; of schools, x, 1–2, 8, 22, 156, 161–2

Ballet, 19

Basic skills, 63–5, 129

'Basics', the, 152–4, 159, 161

Behavioural objectives, *see* Objectives, behavioural

Benevolence, 79–83, 101, 103

Bradley, F. H., 12

Butler, J., 103

Capitalism, 26, 80, 105–6, 158, 168–9

Children: able, 18, 32–3, 137–8, 159–60; handicapped, 137, 159

Christianity, 78, 88–9, 90, 92, 99; *see also* Religious aims

Citizenship, 107–20, 121, 136

Classes, social: middle class, 18, 26; upper class, 18–19, 114–15; working class, 26; *see also* Elitism

Commitment, 56–7, 60, 121, 160–1

Communities, small, 90–2, 108–11, 113

Compulsion, *see* Education, compulsory

Concepts, 25–6, 74–5, 131, 157–8

Conceptual analysis, x, 3–6

Conflicts, 49, 52, 59, 67, 93–7, 111, 119–20, 123, 126

Cooper, D. E., 18

Cultural relativism, *see* Relativism, cultural

Curriculum: school, ix, 63–5, 88–9, 125, 145, 149–62; continuity in, 156–7; control of, x, 1–2, 8, 22, 130, 154–6, 161–2; 'Core', 152–4

Darwin, C., 13

Dearden, R. F., 26, 70, 71

Democracy, 22, 116–20, 124, 148, 157, 162, 168–9; participatory, 2, 116, 143–4, 148, 169; work-place, 106–7, 116, 124, 143–4, 148, 168–9

Development, *see* Growth

Dewey, J., 13, 14

Dickens, C., 90, 142

Dispositions, 5, 58–60, 62, 126, 127, 131; intellectual, 126–7; moral, 70, 71; political, 117; *see also* Virtues

Downie, R., *et al.*, 4, 5, 11, 21–2, 71

Ecology, 124

Economic aims, 61–8, 104–7, 152; *see also* Vocational aims

Economics, 117, 123, 164

Edgley, R., 61

Education: adult, 5, 136; child-centred, 8, 25, 27, 30–7, 69–70; compulsory, 130–6, 138, 150–2, 158–61; concept of, 3–6, 10, 63, 131–2, 164; liberal, 70, 113, 126–7; lifelong, 125, 129–36; vocational, *see* Vocational aims

Education Act (1918), 136

Egoism, 75, 79, 82–7, 91, 94–5, 97, 102–3, 107, 128–9; *see also* Amoralism

Elitism, 17–21, 113–18, 138, 159
English, 152–3
Ethos: of school, 78, 145, 147–9, 151, 155, 163; of society, 87, 88, 93, 141–5, 151, 155, 167
Evolution, 13, 32–3, 123
Examinations, 20, 24, 65, 161
Excellence, 17–21, 36, 136
Extrinsic aims, 2, 4, 5, 21, 22

Family, the, *see* Parents
Foreign languages, 152–3
Forster, E. M., 77
Fraternity, 110, 115–17
Freud, S., 97

Geography, 66, 123–4, 157
God, *see* Religious aims; Christianity
Goethe, J. W. von, 44
Good: common, 69, 72–7, 111; of the pupil, *see* Pupil-centred aims; of society, 21–2, chs 4 and 5 *passim*
Goods: basic, 27–30, 58, 99–100; intrinsic, 30–57, 58, 100
Gordon, P., 12, 73, 90
'Great Debate' (1976), 152
Green, T. H., 12, 13, 101, 112
Growth, 13, 14, 25

Habermas, J., 106
Hansard Society, 66
Happiness, 24, 37–9, 98
Hargreaves, D. H., 72
Headteachers, 148, 156, 161–2
Health Education, 29
Hegel, G. W. F., 11, 12, 22, 44, 90, 93, 109, 110, 142
Herder, 44
Hirst, P. H., 70
History, 66, 123, 157, 164
Human nature, 12, 30, 48–9, 53–4, 74–5, 117, 160–1
Humboldt, W. von, 44–5
Huxley, A., 38

Idealism, Hegelian, 11–13, 73, 90–2, 108, 110–11
Impartiality, 85, 88, 91, 100, 102, 107, 136
Income distribution, 142–4
Individuality, 2, 7, 8, 25, 31–35, 44, 69, 70, 136
Indoctrination, 26, 34, 40, 45, 92, 100, 111, 125–9, 166–7

Integration, 50, 58–9, 67, 94–8, 123, 133, 160–1, 163–4
Intrinsic aims, 2–5, ch. 2 *passim*, 63, 121, 122

Joseph, Sir K., 147

Kant, I., 93
Kantianism, 78, 88
Knowledge: in education, 4, 58–9, 62, 71, 121–4; for its own sake, 1, ch. 2 *passim*, 122, 126, 132, 146, 163–4; forms of, 10, 69, 70, 71, 121–4

Learning, 25
Liberty, 46, 134–5, 159
Lifelong education, *see* Education, lifelong
Life-plan, 45–6, 56–62, 92–5, 98, 123–5, 126, 133–4, 136, 163
Literature, 142, 163
Loudfoot, E., *see* Downie, R., *et al.*

Mabbott, J. D., 110
McCrum, M., 21
MacIntyre, A., 14–16, 21
Mackie, J. L., 90
Marx, K., 44, 142
Marxism, 27, 145
Mathematics, 152–3
Means to ends, 14–16, 18, 28, 123
Media, the, 142–4
Meritocracy, 18, 19
Micro-chip revolution, 29
Midgley, M., 49
Mill, J. S., 44
Mixed ability teaching, 37, 137–8
Moral aims, 3, 5, 61, 67, 68–103, ch. 5 *passim*, 121
Moral experts, 114–16
Morality: autonomous, 92–103, 114, 116; concrete, 90–2; minimalist, 78–88, 92, 100, 102, 105, 142; universalistic, 88–90, 92, 100; *see also* Understanding, moral
Moulding, 125–9

Nation, 111–12
Nationalism, 107, 112
Naturalism, 31, 32, 41–2, 53, 166
Nature, 12, 13, 30, 31–5, 37, 42
Nunn, T. P., 7, 8, 20, 30, 32, 44, 47, 69, 70, 73

Obedience, 104–5, 107, 127–8, 146
Objectives: behavioural, 6, 7; terminal, 125, 129–30, 149–54, 162
Objectivity, 125–9
Organisation: of industry, 59, 62, 66, 105–7, 124, 142–4, 168–9; of schools, 62, 88–9, 148

Parents, 1, 23, 33–4, 72, 74, 165–7
Passmore, J., 167–8
Personal autonomy, *see* Autonomy, personal
Peters, R. S., 6
Philosophy, 115, 117, 123–4, 164
Philosophy of education, x, xi, 27, 164
Piaget, J., 158
Plato, 113–15, 117–18, 136
Pleasure, 38–9
Polis, the, 109
Political education, 66, 116–20, 169
Popper, K., x, 168
Post-reflective desire-satisfaction, 39–57
Poverty, world, *see* Rich and poor countries
Principles of procedure, 6, 7
Progressivism, *see* Education, child-centred
Psychology of education, x, 27, 30, 158, 164
Pupil-centred aims, 19, 22, chs 3 and 4 *passim*, 107, 121, 122

Racial discrimination, 85
Rawls, J., 39, 40, 47–9
Relativism, cultural, 26–7, 127–8
Religious aims, 12, 13, 30–1, 33, 37, 39, 44, 47, 53, 73, 76, 123, 126–7, 146; *see also* Christianity
Rich and poor countries, 73–4, 78, 81–3, 87, 91, 101, 138–9
Robbins Report (1963), 163–4
Rote-learning, 62, 64
Rousseau, J.-J., 44

Schools: 1, 3, 129–30, 145–62; autonomy of, *see* Autonomy, of schools; comprehensive, 18, 113–14, 146–7, 165; continuation, 136, 151, 160, 162; grammar, 17, 113, 146; independent, 17, 113, 146; primary, 3, 24, 37, 63–4, 146, 156–7; public, 18, 21, 113, 146; secondary, 3, 23–4, 64, 66, 156–7; secondary modern, 18, 114, 146

Schools, Council ix, 8
Science, 2, 14, 117, 152–3, 155, 157
Selection, 17–21, 146
Self-creation, 44–7, 48, 54–5
Self-determination, 34; *see also* Autonomy, personal
Self-expression, 45
Self-realisation, 12, 13, 25, 98
Sex roles, 126, 128
Sexual discrimination, 85
Singer, P., 82
Social aims, 3, 25, chs 4 and 5 *passim*, 121
Social change, 145
Social nature of learning, 25
Social studies, 157
Sociology, 123–4
Sociology of education, x, 27, 72, 164
Socrates, 71
Specialisation, 23, 34, 62–5, 114–16, 159–60, 163
State, the, 90, 92, 108–13
Stradling, R., 66

Tawney, R. H., 105
Teachers and politics, 140–5
Teacher education, 3, 25, 72, 164–5
Telfer, E., *see* Downie, R., *et al.*
Totalitarianism, 107–9, 168

Understanding: breadth of, 58–9, 62, 113–18, 121–4, 126, 149; moral, 69–71, 124; *see also* Knowledge
Uniformity, 125–6
Universities, 3, 20, 139, 162–4
Upbringing, 5, 131–4
Utilitarianism, 14, 78, 88, 90
Utopianism, 167–9

Virtues, 70, 104, 121–3, 127–8
Vocational aims, 21, 23, 29, 61–8, 101–2, 104–7, 113, 118, 124, 132, 146, 158; *see also* Economic aims
Voluntary activities, 132, 135, 138, 150–1, 158–61

Warnock Report, 137
White, J., 12, 21, 26, 36, 39, 73, 90, 153, 156
White, P., 106, 116, 148
Whitehead, A. N., ix
Work aims, *see* Economic aims; Vocational aims